N. Mangan - Senior Social Worker

Department of Health and Social Services

MENTAL HEALTH (NORTHERN IRELAND) ORDER 1986

Code of Practice

BELFAST: HMSO

© *Crown copyright 1992*
First published 1992
Third impression 1993
Applications for reproduction should be made to HMSO
ISBN 0 337 07714 2

PREFACE

This Code of Practice was prepared in accordance with Article 111 of the Mental Health (Northern Ireland) Order 1986 by the Department of Health and Social Services after consulting the Mental Health Commission for Northern Ireland and such other bodies as appeared to the Department to be concerned.

CONTENTS

		Page
1.	**INTRODUCTION**	
	1.1 Purpose of the Code	1
	1.4 Scope of the code	2
	1.6 References	2
	1.8 Principles	3
	1.10 Definitions	4
	1.16 Expressions used in the Code	5
2.	**COMPULSORY ADMISSION TO HOSPITAL FOR ASSESSMENT**	
	2.1 Introduction	6
	2.4 Application for admission for assessment	6
	2.7 Choice of applicant	8
	2.8 The nearest relative	8
	2.13 ASW responsibilities	9
	2.21 Medical recommendation	11
	2.26 The application	13
	2.27 Alternatives to application for admission	13
	2.30 Disagreements	14
	2.31 Admission of children and young persons under the age of 18 years	14

			Page
	2.37	Conveyance to hospital	16
	2.39	Conveyance by the nearest relative	16
	2.40	Conveyance by the ASW	17
	2.50	Role of the responsible Board	19
	2.51	Admission procedures	19
	2.52	Receipt and scrutiny of documents	20
	2.57	Medical examination on arrival	21
	2.61	Notifications to Board and Mental Health Commission	22
	2.62	Rectification of applications, recommendations and reports	22
	2.63	Detention for treatment	23
	2.64	Detention of a voluntary patient already in hospital	23
	2.66	Nurse's holding power	24
	2.70	Application for assessment in respect of a patient already in hospital	26
	2.71	Documentation	26
	2.72	Duty to give information to patients and nearest relatives	26
3.	**RECEPTION INTO GUARDIANSHIP**		
	3.1	Introduction	27
	3.3	Components of effective guardianship	27
	3.5	Application for reception into guardianship	28

		Page
3.6	Choice of applicant	28
3.7	The nearest relative	29
3.11	ASW responsibilities	30
3.14	Medical recommendations	30
3.16	The application	31
3.18	Notifications to Mental Health Commission	31
3.19	Rectification of guardianship applications and recommendations	31
3.20	Role of the Board	32
3.21	Powers of the guardian	33
3.25	Alternatives to guardianship application	35

4. PATIENTS CONCERNED IN CRIMINAL PROCEEDINGS OR UNDER SENTENCE

4.1	Introduction	36
4.5	Hospital admissions ordered by a Court	37
4.6	Role of the responsible Board	39
4.8	Boards' Designated Officers	40
4.9	Duties of the doctor giving medical evidence to the Court	40
4.11	Medical assessment of the accused person	41
4.12	Arrangements for the accused person's hospital care	41

		Page
4.16	Boards' representations in Court	42
4.20	Arrangements for admission	43
4.22	Admissions directed by the Secretary of State	44
4.24	Admission	45
4.25	Conveyance to hospital	45
4.27	Admissions to special hospitals	46
4.30	Admissions from special hospitals	47
4.33	Guardianship ordered by a Court	47

5. TREATMENT AND CARE

5.1	Introduction	49
5.3	Principles of treatment	49
5.4	Treatment plans	50
5.8	Consent to treatment	51
5.10	Treatment requiring consent and a second opinion	52
5.12	Treatment requiring consent or a second opinion	53
5.14	Treatment without consent	53
5.19	Consent by children and young persons under the age of 18 years	55
5.22	Withdrawal of consent	57
5.23	Urgent treatment	57

			Page
	5.24	Consent by relatives	58
	5.25	Treatment for physical illness	58
	5.26	Review of treatment	58
	5.27	Conduct presenting particular problems of management	58
	5.29	Causes of behaviour problems	59
	5.30	General preventative measures	59
	5.31	Dealing with violence	60
	5.32	Restraint	61
	5.33	Policy on physical restraint	61
	5.38	Procedural steps for physical restraint	62
	5.43	Personal searches	63
	5.45	Locked ward doors on open wards	64
	5.47	Time out	65
	5.49	Seclusion	65
	5.53	Special accommodation of dangerous patients	66

GLOSSARY 67

INDEX OF STATUTORY REFERENCES 69

INDEX 72

1. INTRODUCTION

Purpose of the Code

1.1 Article 111 of the Mental Health (Northern Ireland) Order 1986 (referred to throughout the Code as 'the Order') requires the Department of Health and Social Services (the Department) to prepare, and from time to time revise, a Code of Practice to be published for the guidance of Health and Social Services Boards, Board staff and others in respect of various matters dealt with in the Order. Article 111(1) defines the purpose of the Code as being:

" (a) for the guidance of medical practitioners, Boards, staff of hospitals and approved social workers in relation to the admission of patients to hospitals and the reception of patients into guardianship under this Order; and

(b) for the guidance of medical practitioners and members of other professions in relation to the medical treatment of patients suffering from mental disorder."

Article 111(2) states:

"The code shall, in particular, specify forms of medical treatment in addition to any specified by regulations made for the purposes of Article 63 which in the opinion of the Department give rise to special concern and which should accordingly not be given by a medical practitioner unless the patient has consented to the treatment ..... ".

Article 63 provides that the Department may by regulation specify forms of treatment requiring both the patient's consent and a second medical opinion.

1.2 The Order does not impose a legal duty to comply with the Code but the fact that the Code had not been followed could be referred to in evidence in legal proceedings.

1.3 As required by the Order, the Department will keep the Code under review and will revise it as appropriate in the light of experience.

Scope of the Code

1.4 The scope of the Code is prescribed by the provisions of Article 111 of the Order and the guidance it contains does not extend beyond the matters specified in that Article. The Code is intended to be complementary to the Order, which should always be referred to for its precise terms; and to the Guide to the Order published by the Department in 1986 (referred to throughout the Code as 'the Guide').

1.5 The Code does not purport to be all-embracing. Its intention is to provide guidance in straightforward language on matters of day to day practice which it would not be appropriate to deal with in primary or secondary legislation. It offers advice on what is generally agreed to be good professional practice in relation to the procedures laid down in the Order. The Department hopes that this will enable members of different professional groups to work together on practical issues that may straddle professional boundaries. It is not concerned with questions of professional judgment which are more appropriately dealt with in clinical and other text books. The Code applies to all patients including those under 18 years. Where specific guidance in respect of younger patients is considered appropriate this is provided.

References

1.6 Appropriate provisions of the Order and corresponding sections of the Guide are referred to throughout the Code by Article and paragraph numbers respectively. All professionals concerned with the operation of the Order should be familiar with the provisions of the Order and sections of the Guide relative to their duties and responsibilities. Other legislative provisions referred to in the text are identified. All references to legislative provisions are listed in the Index of Statutory References.

1.7 References to "Forms" are references to the forms prescribed by Regulation 7 of the Mental Health (Nurses, Guardianship, Consent to Treatment and Prescribed Forms) Regulations (Northern Ireland) 1986 as amended by the Mental Health (Nurses, Guardianship, Consent to Treatment and Prescribed Forms)(Amendment) Regulations (Northern Ireland) 1992. A complete set of the forms is also contained in Appendix 1 to the Guide.

Principles

1.8 The Code must be read with regard to the broad principles that people suffering from mental disorder should:

- be treated and cared for in such a way as to maintain their dignity;

- receive respect for and consideration of their individual qualities and background - social, cultural, and religious;

- have their needs taken fully into account notwithstanding the fact that, within available resources, it may not always be practicable to meet them;

- receive any necessary treatment or care with the least degree of control and segregation consistent with their safety and the safety of others;

- be discharged from any form of constraint or control to which they are subject under the Order immediately this is no longer necessary;

- be treated or cared for in such a way as to promote their self-determination and encourage personal responsibility to the greatest possible degree consistent with their needs, wishes and abilities.

1.9 This means, in particular, that all individuals should be as fully involved as practicable, consistent with their needs and wishes, in the formulation and delivery of their care and treatment. They should be informed about the nature, purpose and likely outcome of any proposed treatment. This applies equally to young patients and to patients who are receiving care or treatment on a compulsory basis. Where physical difficulties such as hearing impairment impede such involvement, reasonable steps should be taken to attempt to overcome them. It means that patients should have their legal rights drawn to their attention, consistent with their capacity to understand them. Where they cannot understand, their rights should be explained to their carers, relatives or friends as appropriate. Finally, it means that, when treatment or care is provided in conditions of security, patients should be subject only to the level of security appropriate to their individual needs and only for so long as it is required.

Definitions

1.10   The Order makes provision with respect to the detention, guardianship, care and treatment of patients suffering from mental disorder. "Mental disorder" and related expressions are defined in Article 3 for the purposes of the Order. The definitions are not meant to delimit psychiatric practice outside the terms of the Order. For example, the exclusions in Article 3(2) mean that a person cannot be compulsorily admitted to hospital under the terms of the Order by reason only of personality disorder (paragraph 14 of the Guide) but that does not mean that someone with personality disorder may not be offered hospital admission for assessment and treatment on a voluntary basis.

1.11   It is not obligatory for the expression "mental disorder" to be used in psychiatric practice only in accordance with the legal definition. To avoid confusion, however, it is generally better to use some other term for conditions which fall outside this definition.

1.12   "Mental disorder" is defined in Article 3 as meaning "mental illness, mental handicap and any other disorder or disability of mind". "Mental illness" and "mental handicap" are then defined individually. The great majority of cases to which the Order applies will fall into one or other of these categories. There may occasionally be a case to which the Order should apply and which falls within the general definition, but which may not exactly fit the definition of either "mental illness" or "mental handicap". An example would be a person who had sustained brain damage in adult life causing a disability similar to that defined within "severe mental handicap" and who satisfied the other criteria of the Order. In such a case, the apparent severe mental handicap is not strictly speaking "a state of arrested or incomplete development of mind". The effect of including "any other disorder or disability of mind" in the general definition of "mental disorder" is to avoid semantic difficulties of this kind when cases, which properly and necessarily fall within the terms of the Order, are being considered. This does not mean that all patients with brain damage should be treated or managed within a particular regime. Brain damage does not always cause intellectual impairment: it can result in various forms of mental disturbance. The nature of the mental disorder will determine the appropriate regime of treatment or management.

1.13   The definitions of "severe mental handicap" and "severe mental impairment" include the term "severe impairment of intelligence and social functioning". That is not meant to restrict these definitions to persons whose intelligence level as measured by psychological tests falls below a particular figure. Assessment should take into account the total impairment both of intelligence and of social functioning.

1.14   The English and Scottish legislation contain definitions of "mental disorder" which are broadly compatible, but not identical, with those in the Order and with each other. The definition in the Mental Health Act 1983 includes "psychopathic disorder"; the Mental Health (Scotland) Act 1984 does not define "mental illness" in detail.

1.15   Article 2 of the Order defines "patient" as a person suffering or appearing to be suffering from mental disorder. The word "patient" should be given the same interpretation in the Code.

Expressions used in the Code

1.16   Medical practitioners appointed by the Mental Health Commission for the purposes of Part II of the Order and Part IV of the Order are commonly known as Part II and Part IV doctors respectively and are referred to as such throughout the Code.

1.17   The responsible medical officer (RMO) is the Part II doctor in charge of the patient's assessment or treatment (or who provides certain medical recommendations required by the Order for the purposes of guardianship).

1.18   Approved social workers (ASWs) are social workers specially trained in dealing with persons who are suffering from mental disorder and appointed by a Board to act as an ASW for the purposes of the Order.

1.19   The glossary defines some of the expressions and words used in the Code.

1.20   Solely to facilitate drafting, the male gender has been used throughout the Code, but the guidance it contains in its references to patients, professional staff and others applies equally to both males and females.

2. COMPULSORY ADMISSION TO HOSPITAL FOR ASSESSMENT

Introduction

2.1   Part II of the Order sets out the circumstances in which, and the procedures through which, mentally disordered persons can be compulsorily admitted to and detained in hospital. It does not, however, deal with admissions through the Courts or transfers from prisons or remand centres, which are covered in Part III.

2.2   The Order makes a very clear distinction between admission to hospital for assessment and detention in hospital for treatment. The distinction is emphasised by the fact that where the assessment is not followed by detention for treatment the assessment period can be disregarded for certain purposes (Article 10 and paragraph 45 of the Guide).

2.3   The admission for assessment procedure is initiated by the applicant with the support of a medical recommendation. The procedure is laid down in Articles 4 to 8 of the Order and explained in paragraphs 18 to 24 of the Guide. Detention for treatment is initiated by a Part II doctor on completion of the assessment process, and the criteria are stringent. The procedure is laid down in Articles 12 and 13 of the Order and explained in paragraphs 46 to 50 of the Guide.

Application for admission for assessment

2.4   The application, founded on a medical recommendation, is central to the admission for assessment procedure. Applications and medical recommendations must be made on the appropriate prescribed forms, and care must be taken to ensure that these are completed correctly. While inaccuracies may be subsequently corrected, any significant irregularity in the documentation may invalidate the authority to admit the patient (Article 11). The scrutiny and amendment of documents is dealt with in paragraphs 2.52 to 2.56 of the Code.

2.5   It is good practice for the professionals involved in the application for admission to be present at the same time (although it may be advantageous for each to interview the patient separately). Everyone involved should be aware of the need to provide mutual support. They should also, where there is a risk of the patient causing serious physical harm, consider calling for police assistance and should know how to use that assistance to minimise the risk of violence.

2.6   Good communication with the patient is essential. In particular:

- where the patient has difficulty either in hearing or speaking, or does not speak English, the assistance of staff with specialist communication skills, such as professional interpreters, should be considered;

- the potential disadvantages of a patient's relative being asked to interpret should be borne in mind;

- where the patient is still unwilling or unable to communicate adequately (despite assistance from interpreters) the decision to proceed will have to be based on whatever information can be obtained from other sources;

- it is not desirable for a patient to be interviewed through a closed door or window except where this is necessary to avoid serious risk to other people. Where there is no immediate risk of physical danger to the patient or to others, powers in the Order to secure access (Article 129) should be considered;

- where the patient is under the effects of sedative medication, or the short-term effects of drugs or alcohol, the interview should be postponed, unless it is not possible because of the patient's disturbed behaviour and the urgency of the case. If it is not realistic to wait, the decision to proceed with the application will have to be based on whatever information can be obtained from all reliable sources;

- the patient should ordinarily be given the opportunity of being interviewed in private, but, if there is a risk of physical violence, the doctor and the applicant can insist on another person being present. If the patient would like another person (for example a friend) to be with him during the interview and any subsequent action which may be taken, he should be assisted in securing that person's attendance unless the urgency of the case or some other proper reason makes it inappropriate to do so.

Choice of applicant

2.7   Application for admission to hospital for assessment may be made by:

- the patient's nearest relative (Article 5(1)(a));

- an ASW (Article 5(1)(b)); or

- a person appointed by the County Court to act as the nearest relative (Article 36).

The nearest relative

2.8   The nearest relative is defined in Article 32 of the Order by reference to a list of relationships in paragraph (1) of that Article, a caring relative taking priority over a non-caring relative (whatever his position on the list). Guidance on how the nearest relative is determined is set out in paragraphs 110 to 112 of the Guide and on the back of the application form (Form 1). He has an important part to play in the application to admit to hospital even if he is not the applicant. He is normally the person who is closest to the patient and will usually be aware of the circumstances surrounding the possible need for admission.

2.9   The doctor should ensure that the nearest relative is aware that he can ask for an ASW to consider making the application. Where the nearest relative is proposing to act as the applicant, the professionals involved in the case should offer him any assistance or advice required. That advice should include such elements of the guidance for ASWs in paragraphs 2.13 to 2.20 of the Code as are appropriate. The nearest relative should also be made aware of the relevant form (Form 1) and how it should be completed. Alternatives to compulsory admission, such as voluntary admission, guardianship, or continuing medical, nursing and social work help outside hospital, should be discussed with him.

2.10   There will, of course, be occasions when the nearest relative does not wish, or is unable, to make the application. Applying for admission at a time of crisis can be a stressful experience. On occasions an application by the nearest relative may be regarded by the patient as rejection by his family. Where the nearest relative is reluctant to initiate the application procedure, the doctor should consult the ASW and explain, to the nearest relative, the ASW's power to make an application.

2.11   ASWs are qualified to address these relationship and procedural issues. Their role is described more fully below. It is envisaged that, in many cases, the nearest relative will continue to play a significant part in the application process, even where the ASW acts as applicant. However, a nearest relative should not be forced to make an application for admission under the Order because of a delay in obtaining the services of an ASW.

2.12   Boards should aim to provide a 24 hour ASW service. They should issue guidance to ASWs on:

- what amounts to a "request" to consider application from the nearest relative;

- how to respond to repeated requests where the condition of the patient has not changed significantly;

- how to respond to a request made on behalf of a nearest relative by a GP or other professional whether employed in the statutory or voluntary sector.

ASW responsibilities

2.13   Article 40 of the Order places a duty on the ASW to make an application where he is satisfied that an application ought to be made and that it is necessary or proper for the application to be made by him. The practical guidance in this part of the Code applies where the ASW is acting under Article 40 but is generally applicable where he is considering an application at the request of the nearest relative.

2.14   To satisfy himself that it is necessary and proper for an application to be made the ASW should interview the patient in person. At the start of the interview he should identify himself to the patient and to members of the family and other professionals present; explain in clear terms his role and the purpose of his visit; and check that the other professionals have explained their roles. ASWs should at all times carry documents identifying themselves as ASWs.

2.15 Paragraph 120 of the Guide gives details of certain requirements in the interview. The general guidance given in paragraph 2.5 of the Code should also be observed.

2.16 The ASW must attempt to identify the patient's nearest relative and ensure that his statutory obligations to the nearest relative are fulfilled. In addition, the ASW should where possible -

 a. ascertain the nearest relative's views about the patient's needs and his (the relative's) own needs in relation to the patient; and

 b. inform the nearest relative of the reasons for considering an application for admission under the Order and the effects of making such an application.

2.17 If the nearest relative objects to an application being made and the ASW wishes to proceed with the application, he must consult a second ASW before he makes the application (Article 5(4)). The second ASW should interview the patient and record his conclusions. If after consultation the first ASW decides to proceed, he must record the nearest relative's objection on the application for assessment. Alternatively he may apply to the County Court to have an acting nearest relative appointed on the grounds that the nearest relative has unreasonably objected to the making of an application (Article 36(3)(c)).

2.18 The ASW should take into account any wishes expressed to him by relatives of the patient and any other relevant circumstances when deciding whether or not to make an application (Article 40(1)(b)). It will be appropriate in certain cases to have regard to any views expressed by particularly close friends.

2.19 The ASW should consult the doctor in attendance and whenever possible other professionals who have been involved with the patient's care, for example home care staff, community psychiatric nurses (CPNs) or community mental handicap nurses (CMHNs).

2.20 When the ASW has decided whether or not he will make an application for admission, he should tell (giving the reason):

- the patient;

- the patient's nearest relative (whenever possible); and

- the doctor(s) involved in the assessment.

Indeed, since the application must be founded on a medical recommendation, it is good practice for both the doctor and the ASW to be present at the same time, although they may wish to interview the patient separately.

Medical recommendation

2.21 The doctor providing the medical recommendation must have examined the patient within the previous 2 days (Article 6). He should, if at all possible, be someone who already knows the patient, and normally the patient's own GP would be the first choice. A partner or locum is not barred from providing the recommendation. A doctor on the staff of the hospital to which the patient is to be admitted cannot provide the recommendation except in a case of urgent necessity (Article 6(c)).

2.22 The criteria for application and medical recommendation for admission for assessment are set out in Article 4(2) and (3) of the Order. Article 4(2) provides that an application may be made in respect of a patient on the grounds that -

> "(a) he is suffering from mental disorder of a nature or degree which warrants his detention in a hospital ....; and
>
> (b) failure to detain him would create a substantial likelihood of serious physical harm to himself or to other persons."

Article 4(3) of the Order provides that an application must be founded on a medical recommendation which includes -

> (a) a statement that, in the opinion of the recommending doctor, the grounds set out in Article 2(a) and (b) apply;

(b) the grounds, including a clinical description of the mental condition, for his opinion that the detention is warranted; and

(c) the evidence for his opinion that failure to detain the patient would create a substantial likelihood of serious physical harm.

Article 2(4) and paragraphs 23 and 24 of the Guide specify the evidence which can be used in determining that there is a substantial likelihood of serious physical harm to himself or to other persons. The assessment of a patient may legitimately involve consideration of any prognosis of future deterioration of the patient's mental health and the known history of his mental disorder. Some examples of what may be considered in assessing the nature of the serious physical harm are:

- uncontrolled over-activity likely to lead to exhaustion;

- gross neglect of hygiene and personal safety which would create a hazard to the patient or others;

- serious and protracted neglect of diet which would lead to malnutrition;

- disinhibited behaviour likely eventually to lead to serious physical harm to the patient, his family or other persons.

2.23   It will be seen that the doctor's responsibility goes beyond diagnostic assessment and includes assessment of the need for detention in hospital. In this he should co-operate with the applicant and consider both the need for detention and the possibility of alternative measures and how they might be taken. When the applicant is the nearest relative, the doctor should advise him that he can discuss the position with an ASW.

2.24   The doctor should specifically address the legal criteria for admission under the Order and set out in his recommendation those aspects of the patient's symptoms and behaviour which satisfy the criteria.

2.25   If an application for assessment is to be made the doctor should contact medical staff in the hospital to which the patient is to be admitted, to discuss any possible difficulties or uncertainties about admission, ensure that a bed will be available and advise of the anticipated time of arrival of the patient at the hospital.

The application

2.26   The application is made on Form 1 by the nearest relative or Form 2 by the ASW, and the doctor's medical recommendation is made on Form 3. As the application must be founded on and accompanied by a medical recommendation, it follows that the doctor should give Form 3 to the applicant. It is important that the correct forms are used and that they are properly completed. Otherwise the receiving hospital may be unable to accept the patient.

Alternatives to application for admission

2.27   Before making a recommendation or proceeding with an application the professionals involved should consider what is needed for the patient's care and protection and (where this applies) for the protection of others. All reasonable options should be considered. Where admission is necessary, generally speaking voluntary admission is to be preferred to compulsory admission under Part II of the Order. But compulsory admission should be considered where the patient's current mental state, together with reliable evidence of past experience, indicates a strong likelihood that he will change his mind about voluntary admission, prior to his actual admission to hospital, with a resulting risk to health and safety.

2.28   If it is decided not to apply for admission, the professionals concerned should decide what action is needed to meet the patient's needs, including the possible provision of other health and social services, and should decide how to implement that action. Other professionals concerned with the patient's care should be fully involved in the taking of such decisions, notably the CPN or CMHN. The professionals should ensure that they, the patient, and (with the patient's consent) the nearest relative and any other closely connected relatives, have a clear understanding of any alternative arrangements and who will be responsible for ensuring that they are put in place. Such arrangements should be recorded in writing and copies made available to all those who need them, subject to the patient's right to confidentiality.

2.29 The ASW should discuss with the patient's nearest relative the reasons for not making an application. The ASW should advise the nearest relative of his rights to apply and suggest that he consult the doctor if he wishes to consider this alternative. Where the ASW has been acting at the request of the nearest relative he must give that relative a written statement of the reasons for not applying for the patient's admission (Article 40(4)). The statement should contain sufficient details to enable the nearest relative to understand the decision whilst at the same time preserving the patient's right to confidentiality. A copy of the statement should be retained by the ASW.

Disagreements

2.30 For an application for assessment to succeed there must be agreement between the applicant and the doctor. Where this is difficult to achieve, consultation with colleagues should be considered, including CPNs, CMHNs and other community care staff. Where there is an unresolved dispute about an application it is essential that the professionals do not abandon the patient and his family. They should explore and determine an alternative plan and ensure that the family is kept informed. Such a plan should identify a named professional who will have responsibility for ensuring its implementation. It should be recorded in writing and copies made available to all those who need them, subject to the needs of confidentiality.

Admission of children and young persons under the age of 18 years

2.31 Part II of the Order applies equally to children and young persons under the age of 18 years. There are, however, a number of issues of particular importance which should be considered when persons under the age of 18 years are admitted to hospital whether on a voluntary basis or on foot of an application for assessment.

2.32 Practice for this age group should be guided by the following principles:

> - young people should be kept as fully informed as possible about their care and treatment; their views and wishes must always be taken into account;

- unless statute specifically overrides, young people should be regarded as having the right to make their own decisions (and in particular treatment decisions) when they have sufficient "under standing and intelligence";

- any intervention in the life of a young person, considered necessary by reason of their mental disorder, should be the least restrictive possible and result in the least possible segregation from family, friends, community and school.

2.33   The legal framework governing the admission to hospital (and treatment) of young people under the age of 18 years (and in particular those under the age of 16 years) is complex and it is the responsibility of all professionals and the Boards to ensure that there is sufficient guidance available to those responsible for the care of children and young people.

2.34   Whenever the admission to hospital (and care and treatment in hospital) of somebody under the age of 16 years is being considered, the following questions (amongst many others) need to be asked:

- who is legally responsible for decisions affecting the child, and who has the authority to make such decisions? Those assuming professional responsibility for the care of a child or young person should always request copies of any statutory orders (wardship, care order, custody order, guardianship order, access arrangements, etc) for reference on the ward;

- if the child is in the custody of parents who are separated, which parent has custody, or is the custody shared?;

- what is the capability of the child to make his own decisions in terms of emotional maturity, intellectual capacity and psychological state?

2.35   Parents or guardians may arrange for the admission of children under the age of 16 years to hospital as voluntary patients. Where a doctor concludes, however, that a child under the age of 16 years has the capacity to make such a decision for himself, the child should not be admitted against his will. Where a child is willing to be admitted, but his parents (or guardian) object, their views should be accorded serious consideration and given due weight. It should be remembered that recourse to law to stop sucn an admission could be sought. Anyone aged 16 to 18 years who is "capable of expressing his own wishes" can admit or discharge himself as a voluntary patient to or from hospital, irrespective of the wishes of his parents or guardian.

2.36   It is always preferable for children and young people admitted to hospital to be accommodated with others of their own age group in children's wards or adolescents' units, separate from adults. If, exceptionally, this is not practicable, discrete accommodation in an adult ward, with facilities appropriate to the needs of children and young people, offers the most satisfactory solution.

Conveyance to hospital

2.37   A duly made application for assessment is sufficient authority for the patient to be conveyed to hospital by the applicant, by a person authorised by him, or by the responsible Board if it is requested to do so by the applicant in a case of difficulty (Article 8(1)). The patient must be admitted to hospital within 2 days, or such longer period not exceeding 14 days as a Part II doctor may certify on Form 4 in exceptional circumstances (Article 8(1) and paragraph 26 of the Guide).

2.38   While being conveyed to hospital the patient is deemed to be in legal custody (Article 131(1)). Should the patient escape while being conveyed to hospital, he may be retaken, and conveyed to the hospital within the time permitted for his admission, by the person who had custody of him immediately before the escape, or any constable or ASW (Article 132(1)).

Conveyance by the nearest relative

2.39   Where the nearest relative is the applicant he should be advised that the assistance of an ASW in conveying the patient to hospital is available on request. Where the nearest relative as the applicant intends to exercise his authority himself, or to authorise some other person unfamiliar with admission procedures to convey the patient, the doctor and other professionals involved in the case should offer him any advice and assistance required. That advice should include the guidance for ASWs set out in the following paragraphs. Where the patient is to be conveyed to hospital by ambulance, the doctor should make the necessary arrangements and explain them to the nearest relative.

Conveyance by the ASW

2.40   Where an ASW is the applicant, has been asked by the nearest relative for assistance or has been appointed by the Board to exercise its duty in a case of difficulty to convey the patient to hospital, the ASW has a professional responsibility for ensuring that all the necessary arrangements are made for the patient's conveyance to hospital and that the patient is properly admitted to the hospital. In planning the patient's conveyance to hospital the ASW should, whilst ensuring that the legalities are observed, favour the most humane and least threatening mode of transport consistent with the needs and the safety of the patient and his escort. Where the decision is that the patient should be conveyed to hospital by ambulance the doctor will normally make the necessary arrangements.

2.41   The ASW is permitted to delegate the task of conveying the patient to another person (eg ambulance personnel or possibly the police). The ASW is, however, ultimately responsible for ensuring that the patient is conveyed in a lawful and humane manner and should be ready to give the necessary guidance to those asked to assist.

2.42   It will often be best to convey the patient by ambulance. The ASW will need to decide if he should accompany the patient. If the patient would prefer to be accompanied by another professional (perhaps better known to him) or by a responsible relative, the ASW may ask that person to escort the patient, provided he is satisfied that in doing so he is not increasing the risk of harm to the patient or others.

2.43   The patient should not be conveyed to hospital by car unless the ASW is satisfied the patient will not endanger himself or others on the journey. There should **always** be an escort for the patient other than the driver.

2.44   If the patient is likely to be violent or dangerous, the police should be asked to help. Such a patient should never be conveyed by private car. Where possible an ambulance should be used, or failing that, a police vehicle. Although the police may have to exercise their duty to protect persons or property while the patient is being conveyed, they should, where this is not inconsistent with their duty, comply with any directions or guidance given by the ASW.

2.45 The ASW should inform the receiving hospital, giving the likely time of arrival, to ensure that the patient is expected and that arrangements have been made for his acceptance and for receiving the admission documents.

2.46 The ASW must ensure that the admission documents arrive at the receiving hospital at the same time as the patient. If the ASW is not travelling in the same vehicle as the patient, the documents should be given to the person authorised to convey the patient with instructions for them to be presented on arrival at the hospital to the nurse in charge of the ward into which the patient is to be admitted.

2.47 If the ASW is not travelling with the patient, he should arrive at the hospital at the same time as the patient or as soon as possible afterwards. He should ensure that the admission documents have been delivered, that the admission of the patient is under way and that any relevant information in his possession is passed to appropriate personnel in the hospital. He should remain in the hospital until the patient has been medically examined.

2.48 Where a patient is admitted for assessment on the application of an ASW who has not consulted the patient's nearest relative, the ASW must inform the nearest relative as soon as is practicable (Article 5(5)). Where a patient who is subject to guardianship under the Order is admitted for assessment, the Board must inform the guardian as soon as is practicable (Article 8(3)).

2.49 A patient who has been sedated **for the purpose of being conveyed to hospital** should be accompanied by a nurse, doctor or ambulance person who is sufficiently skilled in resuscitation techniques and the observation of drowsy or comatose patients.

Role of the responsible Board

2.50 Under Article 8(1)(b) of the Order it is a Board's responsibility to convey a patient to hospital in a case of difficulty. To meet such cases Boards should, in conjunction with other authorities likely to be involved in conveying patients to hospital (eg the police), prepare joint guidance on policy and procedures including:

- a clear statement of the roles and obligations of each authority and its personnel;

- the form of any authorisation to be given by the ASW to others to convey the patient to hospital; and

- guidance to personnel as to their powers in relation to conveying patients to hospital.

Admission Procedures

2.51 A valid application for assessment constitutes authority for the patient not only to be conveyed to hospital but also to be detained there for the purposes of a medical examination (a report of which should be sent to the responsible Board) and of subsequent assessment (Articles 8(2) and 9). The essential procedures to be followed on the patient's arrival at hospital are:

- receipt and scrutiny of the application and medical recommendation;

- acceptance and medical examination of the patient;

- notification of the application and detention for assessment to the Board and the Mental Health Commission.

Proper procedures should be applied for the care of patients' property on admission to hospital.

Receipt and scrutiny of documents

2.52   General Managers are ultimately responsible for establishing the validity of a duly completed application for assessment as authority to detain a patient for medical examination and assessment. They should formally delegate this responsibility to officers who will receive the patient. Normally this duty will fall to the nurse in charge of the ward or unit.

2.53   Responsibility for receiving the patient and checking the application must be assumed by a first level nurse registered in the Register of Nurses, Midwives and Health Visitors in accordance with Regulation 3 of the Mental Health (Nurses, Guardianship, Consent to Treatment and Prescribed Forms) Regulations (Northern Ireland) 1986 (that is, a first level nurse trained in the nursing of persons suffering from mental illness or mental handicap).

2.54   The receiving officer should have delegated authority to ensure that the documents are in order. He should be familiar with the requirements of the Order and be able to refer to an authorised administrative officer in any case where there is doubt about the validity of the documents. Both the receiving officer and the administrative officer should understand what errors can properly be corrected in accordance with Article 11 of the Order (paragraph 2.62 of the Code). This subject is covered in paragraphs 34 to 44 of the Guide.

2.55   Medical recommendations should be examined at the same time as the application. They must be scrutinised to ensure that they show sufficient legal grounds for detention. The clinical description of the patient's mental condition should include a description of his symptoms and of his behaviour, not merely a diagnostic classification. The receiving officer should have ready access to a hospital doctor with delegated responsibility who is familiar with the requirements of the Order and be able to refer to the doctor in any case where there is uncertainty about the medical recommendation accompanying the application for assessment. The doctor making the recommendation will have been in touch with a hospital doctor to arrange for the patient's reception, and that hospital doctor should have advised the receiving officer that the patient is to be admitted and have explained the medical grounds for the recommendation. Ideally he should be the hospital doctor to whom the nurse can refer queries about the medical recommendation. If he will not be that doctor, he should brief colleagues to whom such reference may be made, in anticipation of the arrival at hospital of the patient and the documents. It would be advantageous, when contacting the hospital, for the doctor recommending admission to speak to the doctor who will examine the patient on arrival.

2.56   When the patient is being admitted on the application of an ASW, the person receiving the admission documents should check their accuracy with the ASW.

Medical examination on arrival

2.57   The patient must be medically examined immediately on arrival at the hospital by the RMO, another Part II doctor, or any other doctor on the staff of the hospital (Article 9). The examining doctor should preferably have discussed the case beforehand with the doctor who made the recommendation for admission. Failing this the examining doctor should seek all relevant information from the hospital doctor contacted by the doctor who made the recommendation. This should reduce the likelihood of disagreement on the need to admit the patient for assessment.

2.58   The examining doctor must report the result of his examination to the Board on Form 7 whether his opinion be that the patient should be detained in hospital for assessment, should remain in hospital on a voluntary basis or should not remain in hospital. The patient may be detained for up to 7 days on the opinion of the RMO or another Part II doctor. On the opinion of any other doctor the patient may be detained for a period of up to 48 hours during which he must be examined by the RMO or other Part II doctor who must report to the Board on Form 8. If the examining doctor forms the opinion that detention should continue the patient may be detained for up to 7 days from the date of the first examination. Either way the assessment period cannot exceed 7 days without a further examination. If within the 7 day period a Part II doctor examines the patient and reports to the Board on Form 9, the assessment period may be extended for a further 7 days after the expiration of the first 7 day period. In no circumstances can a patient be detained more than 14 days for assessment.

2.59   Where a patient has been admitted for assessment on the application of his nearest relative the responsible Board must arrange for a social worker to interview the patient and report on the patient's social circumstances to the RMO (Article 5(6)). The RMO should take the social worker's report into account when making his assessment. It is imperative therefore that the report should be available to the RMO as soon as possible within the assessment period.

2.60 The purpose of the application for admission is to permit a comprehensive assessment of the patient to be made in hospital and a decision as to the need for further detention for treatment to be taken on the strength of that assessment. There are obvious objections to anticipating the outcome of the assessment process. A decision to reject the application on examination of the patient on arrival should not, therefore, be taken lightly. Such a decision should only be taken on the judgment of a Part II doctor normally after consultation with, and, if possible the agreement of, the doctor who made the recommendation for admission. An examining doctor who is not a Part II doctor should, therefore, before taking such a decision, consult a Part II doctor. The examining doctor should arrange for the doctor who made the recommendation for admission and the applicant to be informed by letter where the patient is to be detained for assessment or to remain in hospital as a voluntary patient. Where the decision is that the patient should be discharged the examining doctor should immediately inform the doctor who made the application and the latter should, with the other professionals concerned, decide what action is needed to meet the patient's needs, including the possible provision of other health and social services, and decide how to implement that action.

Notifications to Board and Mental Health Commission

2.61 A valid application is authority for the responsible Board to detain the patient in hospital for assessment. Once the hospital has admitted a patient for examination a copy of the application (Form 1 or Form 2) and the medical recommendation (Form 3) should be forwarded to the Board which should immediately send copies to the Mental Health Commission. The examining doctor's report (Form 7) should also, whatever the outcome of his examination, be forwarded to the Board on completion and copied immediately by the Board to the Commission. Any subsequent reports relating to detention for assessment (Forms 8 or 9) should be forwarded on completion to the Board and immediately copied by the Board to the Commission, as should a report on Form 10 relating to detention for treatment (paragraph 2.63 of the Code).

Rectification of applications, recommendations and reports

2.62 Article 11 of the Order provides that an application for assessment, medical recommendation or examining doctor's report found within 14 days of admission to be incorrect or defective, may be corrected within the 14 days.

Where a medical recommendation or report is deemed insufficient to warrant detention the applicant should be informed. Article ll provides that in such circumstances the recommendation or report shall be disregarded but the application shall be deemed to be sufficient if a fresh recommendation or report complying with the provisions of the Order is furnished to the Board. The Mental Health Commission must be informed of any alterations made and sent a copy of any substitution furnished. The authorised administrative officer (paragraph 2.54 of the Code) should ensure that any such corrections are made as required by, and in accordance with, Article 11 of the Order (paragraphs 34 to 44 of the Guide).

Detention for treatment

2.63 The RMO, or another Part II doctor in the absence of the RMO, must examine the patient before the end of the initial 7 day assessment period. If the examining doctor decides that further detention is not necessary the patient will either remain in hospital voluntarily or be discharged. If the doctor decides that the patient should be detained for a further period, that period will commence after the expiry of the first period (Article 9(8)). The patient must be re-examined before the end of the second period. If the examining doctor is then of the opinion that the patient should be detained for treatment, and the criteria of Article 12(1) of the Order are satisfied, the doctor must report to the Board on Form 10 .

Detention of a voluntary patient already in hospital

2.64 Article 7 of the Order provides that an application for assessment may be made in respect of a hospital in-patient who is not liable to be detained under the Order, where it appears to a medical practitioner on the staff of the hospital that an application ought to be made. In effect this allows a patient to be held for up to 48 hours to allow the application to be made.

2.65 Where a doctor is of the opinion that an application for assessment ought to be made in respect of a patient already in hospital including a general hospital (but not an out-patient or someone attending an accident and emergency department) the doctor should, when appropriate, complete Form 5 recording his reasons. Use should only be made of this provision, and Form 5 should only be completed, where there is a possibility that the patient could seek to leave hospital before an application can be made. The Form should not be completed unless at the time there is a genuine intention on the part of the doctor that an application for assessment should be made (paragraph 2.70 of the Code). Once Form 5 has been completed the patient can be held in the hospital for up to 48 hours to permit that to be done. An application for assessment in respect of a voluntary patient may, of course, be made in the normal way without resort to Article 7 of the Order and completion of Form 5.

Nurse's holding power

2.66 A doctor may not always be immediately available when a voluntary patient, undergoing treatment for mental disorder, seeks to leave hospital and cannot be persuaded to stay. In such circumstances, an appropriately qualified nurse may exercise a holding power (provision for which is made in Article 7(3) of the Order) to detain the patient where the nurse is of the opinion that :

- an application for assessment ought to be made in respect of the patient; and

- it is not practicable to secure the immediate attendance of a doctor.

The holding power may be exercised by a first level nurse registered in the Register of Nurses, Midwives and Health Visitors in accordance with Regulation 3 of the Mental Health (Nurses, Guardianship, Consent to Treatment and Prescribed Forms) Regulations (Northern Ireland) 1986 (that is, a first level nurse trained in the nursing of persons suffering from mental illness or mental handicap).

2.67 A suitably qualified nurse should be on all wards where there is a possibility of the nurse's holding power being used. This is most likely to occur on acute admission wards and wards where there are severely disturbed patients. Hospital management should assess the potential for its use elsewhere in the hospital and ensure that appropriate arrangements are in place for a suitably qualified nurse to be available. Clear procedural guidelines should be available to all staff in these settings.

2.68 The decision to exercise the holding power is at the personal discretion of the nurse. He cannot be instructed to exercise this power by anyone else. Before using the power the nurse should assess:

   a. the likely arrival time of the doctor as against the likely intention of the patient to leave. Most patients who express a wish to leave hospital can be persuaded to wait until a doctor arrives, to discuss the matter further. Where this is not possible the nurse must try to predict the impact of any delay upon the patient; and

   b. the consequences of a patient leaving hospital immediately including the harm that might occur to the patient or others taking into account:

   - what the patient says he will do and his known history;

   - the likelihood of the patient committing suicide;

   - the patient's current behaviour and in particular any changes from usual behaviour;

   - the likelihood of the patient behaving in a violent manner;

   - the availability of appropriate accommodation and support in the home;

   - any recently received messages from relatives or friends;

   - any recent disturbance on the ward (which may or may not have involved the patient);

   - any relevant involvement of other patients;

   - any relevant information from other members of the multi-disciplinary team.

2.69 The nurse must record, on Form 6, his opinion that an application for assessment ought to be made. The reasons for invoking the holding power should be entered in the patient's nursing notes. The nurse's holding power starts once he has completed Form 6 and ends 6 hours later or on the earlier arrival of a hospital doctor empowered to report that an application for assessment should be made. Where the doctor is in attendance pursuant to the exercise of the nurse's holding power but is of the opinion that an application for assessment should not be made the patient cannot be held further, and Form 5 should not be completed.

Application for assessment in respect of a patient already in hospital

2.70   So far as possible the application procedures described in paragraphs 2.4 to 2.26 of the Code should be followed. Where practicable the patient's own GP should attend the hospital to give the medical recommendation on which the application would be founded. A doctor on the staff of the hospital in which it is intended the assessment should be carried out cannot give the recommendation except in a case of urgent necessity (Article 6(c)). The Order does not prohibit a doctor on the staff of another hospital from making the medical recommendation, but it is preferable for this to be done by the patient's own GP, or by another practitioner who has previous knowledge of the patient (Article 6(b)).

Documentation

2.71   Forms 6 and 5 should be delivered to the Board as soon as possible, and copied by the Board immediately on receipt to the Mental Health Commission.

Duty to give information to patients and nearest relatives

2.72   The Board must ensure that each detained patient and his nearest relative receive the information to which they are entitled under Article 27 of the Order at the time and in the manner specified in that Article (paragraphs 92 to 97 of the Guide).

3. RECEPTION INTO GUARDIANSHIP

Introduction

3.1   The purpose of guardianship is primarily to ensure the welfare (rather than the medical treatment) of a patient in a community setting where this cannot be achieved without the use of some or all of the powers vested by guardianship. It provides a less restrictive means of offering assistance to a person than, and should be considered as an alternative to, detention in hospital. It enables the establishment of an authoritative framework for working with a patient with a minimum of constraint to help him to achieve as independent a life as possible within the community. Arrangements for giving effect to guardianship should not be unnecessarily complicated. The objective should be simply to ensure that guardianship is used properly and in a positive and flexible manner.

3.2   Part II of the Order sets out the circumstances in which, and the procedures through which, certain mentally disordered persons aged 16 or over may be received into guardianship. Part II does not, however, deal with guardianship orders made by the Courts which are covered in Part III.

Components of effective guardianship

3.3   Where guardianship is used it should be part of an agreed comprehensive care plan drawn up by the professionals who are or who could be involved in the patient's care, and, where appropriate, the patient's nearest relative or other informal carer. The plan should identify the services needed by the patient, including as necessary his care arrangements, appropriate accommodation, his treatment and personal support requirements, and those who have responsibilities under the care plan. It should indicate which of the powers given by guardianship are necessary to achieve the plan. If none of the powers given by guardianship are considered necessary for achieving the patient's welfare, guardianship is inappropriate.

3.4 The following components are necessary for guardianship to be effective:

- a willingness by the guardian to "advocate" on behalf of the patient in relation to those agencies whose services are needed to carry out the care plan;

- readily available support from the Board for the guardian;

- an appropriate place of residence taking into account the patient's needs for support, care, treatment and protection;

- access to necessary day care, education and training facilities as appropriate;

- effective co-operation and communication between all persons concerned in implementing the care plan.

Where the patient is capable of understanding, it is also necessary that there should be a recognition by the patient of the "authority" of the guardian. There must be a willingness on the part of both parties to work together within the terms of the authority which is vested in the guardian by the Order.

Application for reception into guardianship

3.5 The application, founded on 2 medical recommendations and a recommendation by an ASW, is central to the reception into guardianship procedure. The procedure is laid down in Articles 18 to 21 of the Order and explained in paragraphs 74 to 80 of the Guide. Applications and recommendations must be made on the appropriate prescribed forms, and care must be taken to ensure that these are completed correctly.

Choice of applicant

3.6 Application for reception into guardianship may be made by:

- the patient's nearest relative (Article 19(1)(a));

- an ASW (Article 19(1)(b));

- a person appointed by a County Court to act as the nearest relative (Article 36).

The nearest relative

3.7 The nearest relative is defined in Article 32 of the Order by reference to a list of relationships in paragraph (1) of that Article, a caring relative taking priority over a non-caring relative (whatever his position on the list). He has an important part to play in the guardianship application even if he is not the applicant or the person named as the prospective guardian. He is normally the person who is closest to the patient and will usually be aware of the circumstances surrounding the possible need for guardianship. The patient may be required to live with the nearest relative whilst under guardianship.

3.8 Professionals involved in a case should offer to the nearest relative any advice or assistance required where he is proposing to act as the applicant and/or guardian. As applicant he should be made aware of the relevant form (Form 13) and how it should be completed. As prospective guardian he should be advised about the effect of guardianship and the extent and limitations of a guardian's powers (paragraphs 3.21 to 3.24 of the Code).

3.9 The Code envisages that the nearest relative will continue to play a significant part in the reception of patients into guardianship, even where the ASW acts as applicant, except where this is clearly not desirable, for example where the patient has been neglected or abused by the nearest relative. In no circumstances should pressure be brought to bear on the nearest relative to make a guardianship application, act as guardian or participate in the continuing care of the patient whilst the patient is subject to guardianship.

3.10 Where the nearest relative unreasonably objects to the making of a guardianship application the ASW should pursue the application. Alternatively he may apply to the County Court to have an acting nearest relative appointed.

ASW responsibilities

3. 11 ASWs have 2 distinct roles in the application process, and these must be carried out by 2 different ASWs.

3.12 Article 40 of the Order places a duty on the ASW to make a guardianship application where he is satisfied that an application ought to be made and that it is necessary or proper for the application to be made by him. The practical guidance in paragraphs 2.13 to 2.20 of the Code is equally applicable where the ASW is considering making a guardianship application pursuant to his duty under Article 40 and is generally applicable also where he is considering an application at the request of the nearest relative.

3.13 A guardianship application must be founded on a recommendation by an ASW other than the ASW applicant and on 2 medical recommendations. In making a recommendation the ASW has to be reasonably satisfied that reception into guardianship is in the interests of the welfare of the patient. This includes being sure that appropriate facilities are available to give effect to the powers of guardianship, such as a suitable place of residence or adequate arrangements for occupation, education or training.

Medical recommendations

3.14 Two medical recommendations are required and may be made jointly or separately (paragraphs 76 and 77 of the Guide). If the doctors examine the patient separately they must do so within 7 days of each other. Each must sign his recommendation within 2 days of carrying out the examination. One recommendation must be given by a Part II doctor. The other should, if at all possible, be made by the patient's own general practitioner or by a medical practitioner who already knows the patient. Neither recommendation can be made by the prospective guardian.

3.15 The criteria for guardianship application and medical recommendation are set out in Article 18(2) and (3) (a) of the Order. The medical criteria differ from those for application for admission to hospital for assessment in that the patient must be diagnosed as suffering from "mental illness or **severe** mental handicap".

The application

3.16 A guardianship application is made to the responsible Board. The application may name the responsible Board or any other willing person including the applicant as prospective guardian (Article 18(5) and (6)). The application is made on Form 13 by the nearest relative or on Form 14 by the ASW. The medical recommendations may be given jointly on Form 15 or separately on Form 16. The ASW's recommendation is given on Form 17. As the application must be founded on these recommendations Form 15 (or 2 separate Forms 16) and Form 17 must be completed before Form 13 or Form 14. It follows that the completed recommendation forms should be given to the applicant. The correct forms must be used and must be properly completed, if the Board is to be able to grant the application.

3.17 Where a patient is received into guardianship on the application of an ASW who has not consulted the patient's nearest relative, the ASW must inform the nearest relative as soon as is practicable (Article 19(6)).

Notifications to Mental Health Commission

3.18 Where a patient is received into guardianship the Board should forward a copy of the application and the recommendations on which it is founded to the Mental Health Commission (Article 22(5)).

Rectification of guardianship applications and recommendations

3.19 Article 21 of the Order provides that a guardianship application or any recommendation on which it is founded, discovered within 14 days of acceptance by the Board to be incorrect or defective, may be corrected within the 14 days. Where a recommendation is deemed insufficient to warrant reception into guardianship the applicant should be informed. Article 21 provides that in such circumstances the recommendation shall be disregarded but that the application shall be deemed to be sufficient if a fresh recommendation complying with the provisions of the Order is furnished to the Board. The Mental Health Commission must be informed of any alterations made and sent a copy of any substitution furnished.

Role of the Board

3.20 The Mental Health (Nurses, Guardianship, Consent to Treatment and Prescribed Forms) Regulations (Northern Ireland) 1986 govern the exercise by guardians of their powers under the Order and impose duties on guardians and on the Boards in the interests of patients. In pursuance of its powers and duties under the Order and the Regulations each Board should prepare and publish a statement setting out its arrangements for:

- receiving, considering and scrutinising applications for guardianship. Such arrangements should ensure that applications are adequately, but **speedily**, considered;

- ensuring the suitability of any proposed private guardian (ie a guardian other than a Board);

- ensuring that private guardians understand and carry out their statutory powers and duties, including those prescribed in Regulation 4 requiring compliance with Board directions and notification to the Board of particulars relating to the patient;

- ensuring that each patient under guardianship receives, both orally and in writing as soon as practicable and commensurate with his understanding, the information to which he is entitled under Article 27 of the Order, including notification of the provision of the Order under which he is subject to guardianship and the effect of that provision; his rights to apply to the Mental Health Review Tribunal (the patient should also be advised that a named officer of the Board will give any necessary assistance to make such an application); and the effects of the provisions of the Order relating to discharge from guardianship and his right to make representations to the Commission (paragraphs 92 to 97 of the Guide);

- ensuring that each patient's nearest relative is furnished with a statement of his rights and powers under the Order and, subject to the patient's wishes, a copy of any written information given to the patient (paragraph 96 of the Guide);

- monitoring the progress of the guardianship including steps to be taken to fulfil the Board's statutory obligations in relation to guardianship. These statutory obligations include those prescribed in Regulation 5 relating to supervision of private guardians and to visits to patients under guardianship;

- maintaining detailed records relating to patients subject to guardianship;

- reviewing guardianship towards the end of each period;

- complying with the provisions of Article 24 of the Order for discharging patients from guardianship (guardianship should not simply be allowed to lapse when no longer appropriate);

- transferring guardianship from or to the Board, or from one person to another, in accordance with Articles 25 and 28 of the Order. Circumstances in which this would be appropriate are described in paragraphs 86 to 89, 99 and 102 to 105 of the Guide;

- notifying the Mental Health Commission of events prescribed in Regulation 5.

Where the Board is named, and appointed, as guardian it should nominate a professional officer to carry out its duties as guardian.

Powers of the guardian

3.21   Article 22 of the Order gives the guardian power -

"to require the patient to reside at a place specified by the Board or person named as guardian". The patient may be taken to the specified place in furtherance of this requirement if he willingly complies or offers no resistance. However, this power does not provide the legal authority to detain a patient physically in such a place, nor does it authorise the removal of a patient against his will. If the patient is absent without leave from the specified place, he may be returned to it within 28 days by those authorised to do so under Article 29(2) and (3) of the Order;

> "to require the patient to attend at places and times so specified for the purpose of medical treatment, occupation, education or training". If the patient refuses to attend the guardian is not authorised to use force to secure such attendance, nor does the Order enable medical treatment to be administered in the absence of the patient's consent;

> "to require access to the patient to be given at any place where the patient is residing to any medical practitioner, approved social worker or other person so specified". A refusal without reasonable cause to permit an authorised person to have access to the patient is an offence under Article 125 of the Order. Neither the guardian nor any authorised person can use force to secure entry".

If the patient consistently resists the exercise of the guardian's powers, it can be concluded that guardianship is not the most appropriate form of care for that person and guardianship should be discharged.

3.22 Guardianship does not restrict the patient's access to hospital services on a voluntary basis. Furthermore, guardianship can remain in force if the patient is admitted to hospital for assessment under Article 4 of the Order (paragraph 106 of the Guide). However, it ceases to have effect if the patient is detained for treatment under Article 12 of the Order. If guardianship is considered to be appropriate when the patient is discharged following detention for treatment, a fresh application for guardianship is required.

3.23 It is possible for a person subject to guardianship under Part II of the Order to be transferred into the guardianship of another Board or person approved by such Board (Article 28).

3.24 Where an adult is assessed as requiring residential care but due to mental incapacity is unable to make a decision as to whether he wishes to be placed in residential care, those who are responsible for his care should consider the applicability and appropriateness of guardianship for providing a framework within which decisions about his current and future care can be planned. Guardianship does not, however, confer powers to compel the admission of an unwilling person into residential care.

Alternatives to guardianship application

3.25   Before making a recommendation or guardianship application the professionals involved should consider all reasonable alternatives for providing for the patient's care and protection. The practical guidance in paragraphs 2.27 and 2.28 of the Code is equally applicable when guardianship is being contemplated.

4. PATIENTS CONCERNED IN CRIMINAL PROCEEDINGS OR UNDER SENTENCE

Introduction

4.1   Part III of the Order provides for the admission to hospital or placement under guardianship of persons concerned in criminal proceedings or under sentence. The Department's role and responsibilities under the provisions of Part III have been delegated to Boards by the Functions of Health and Social Services Boards (No. 1) Direction (Northern Ireland) 1973, as amended by the Functions of Health and Social Services Boards (No. 1) Direction (Northern Ireland) 1986.

4.2   People who are mentally disordered are particularly vulnerable when in custody. All professional staff should take this into account in dealing with accused or convicted prisoners, not forgetting the possibility of self-injury or suicide.

4.3   Those subject to criminal proceedings are entitled to any necessary psychiatric assessment and treatment. Although psychiatric treatment is available to persons in prison custody, there are limitations to the treatment which can be provided in prison, and a prison hospital or a prison psychiatric unit is not a hospital as defined in the Order.

4.4   Part III of the Order provides that in certain circumstances an accused person may, by order of a Court, be admitted to hospital on grounds of mental illness or severe mental impairment or placed under guardianship on grounds of mental illness or severe mental handicap. Part III also provides that in certain circumstances a person convicted of an offence, or on remand, may by direction of the Secretary of State for Northern Ireland be admitted to hospital on grounds of mental illness or severe mental impairment.

Hospital admissions ordered by a Court

4.5 A Court may order a person's admission to hospital under the following Articles of the Order:

i. Article 42 - Remand for report on accused's mental condition.

The Crown Court or a Magistrates' Court may remand to hospital a person, who has been accused of an offence, for a report on his mental condition. Before exercising the powers in Article 42 the Court must be satisfied that there is reason to suspect mental illness or severe mental impairment. Oral evidence by a Part II doctor is required. The remanded person must be admitted to hospital within 7 days of the date of the remand. Anyone so remanded has the status of a patient compulsorily detained in hospital, except that the right to give treatment without consent conveyed in Article 69 does not apply. He may be kept in hospital for up to 28 days, and thereafter may be further remanded by the Court for similar periods up to a maximum of 12 weeks.

ii. Article 43 - Remand for treatment.

The Crown Court may remand an accused person to hospital for treatment. Before exercising the powers in Article 43 the Court must be satisfied that the accused person is suffering from mental illness or severe mental impairment. Oral evidence by a Part II doctor, and oral or written evidence by one other medical practitioner, is required. The remanded person must be admitted to hospital within 7 days of the date of the remand. Anyone so remanded has the status of a detained patient. He may be kept in hospital for up to 28 days, and thereafter may be further remanded by the Court for similar periods up to a maximum of 12 weeks.

iii. Articles 44 and 47 - Hospital order and restriction order.

The Crown Court or a Magistrates' Court may (by a hospital order) order the hospital admission of a person convicted of an imprisonable offence (Article 44(1)). A Magistrates' Court may also make a hospital order in respect of an accused person without conviction if it is satisfied that he committed the act of which he is accused (Article 44(4)). Either Court may in addition make an order restricting discharge from hospital (Article 47), either for a specified period or without limit of time. Before exercising the powers in Articles 44 and 47 the Court must be satisfied that the convicted or accused person is suffering from mental illness or severe mental impairment. Oral evidence by a Part II doctor, and written or oral evidence by another medical practitioner, are required. The subject of a hospital order must be admitted to hospital within 28 days of the date of the order. The subject of a hospital order has the status of a detained patient. If there is a restriction order, the Secretary of State will exercise authority, through the Northern Ireland Office, over the patient's discharge or leave of absence from hospital and will require periodic reports on the patient from the RMO.

iv. **Article 45 - Interim hospital order.**

The Crown Court or a Magistrates' Court may (by an interim hospital order) order the hospital admission of a person convicted of an imprisonable offence, if it has reason to suppose but is not certain at the time that a hospital order under Article 44 is justified. Before exercising the power in Article 45 the Court must be satisfied that the convicted person is suffering from mental illness or severe mental impairment. Oral evidence by a Part II doctor, and oral or written evidence by another medical practitioner, is required. The subject of an interim order must be admitted to hospital within 28 days of the date of the order. The effect of an interim order is similar to that of a hospital order, except that the Court specifies its duration, which must not exceed 12 weeks. The Court may renew an interim order on expiry for periods of up to 28 days, but the maximum period of an interim hospital order (with renewals) must not exceed 6 months. It may be superseded by a hospital order made under Article 44.

v. **Article 49 - Unfitness to be tried.**

Where the Crown Court decides that an accused person is unfit to be tried it will order that person to be admitted to hospital. The question of fitness to be tried is decided by a jury, or a judge in the case of a Diplock Court, and there is no specific requirement in the Order for medical evidence. Usually the Court will wish to hear medical evidence. Although there is no right under Article 49 for a Board to make representations to the Court concerning such cases, the appropriate Board should be prepared to offer advice to the Court if required. The subject of such an order must be admitted to hospital within 28 days of the date of the order. The effect of such an order is the same as that of a hospital order (Article 44) together with a restriction order made without limitation of time (Article 47).

vi. Article 50 - Not guilty on the ground of insanity.

Where the Crown Court finds that a person committed the offence with which he has been charged but was an insane person at the time, the Court will order his admission to hospital. Article 50 requires the Court to be given "evidence ..... that the person charged was an insane person at the time the offence was committed". It does not specify the nature of that evidence, but in practice the evidence will normally be given by at least one psychiatrist. Although there is no right under Article 50 for a Board to make representations to the Court concerning such cases, the appropriate Board should be prepared to offer advice to the Court if required. The subject of such an order must be admitted to hospital within 28 days of the date of the order. The effect of such an order is the same as that of a hospital order (Article 44) with a restriction order made without limit of time (Article 47).

Role of the responsible Board

4.6   In all cases, the decision as to whether the person in court should be admitted to hospital lies solely with the Court. However, a Court cannot remand a person to hospital for assessment or treatment, nor make a hospital order or interim hospital order, unless the Board which will be responsible for implementing the order has been given an opportunity to make representations to the Court in accordance with Articles 42(4), 43(3), 44(5) and 45(3) of the Order: the Department's statutory role in making representations has been delegated to the Boards, as explained in paragraph 4.1 of the Code. No similar opportunity is provided by the Order in respect of orders made under Articles 49 and 50 though the Court may invite the Board to make representations and Boards should, therefore, always be prepared for this eventuality.

4.7   Boards are responsible for securing admission when this is ordered by a Court. By availing itself of the opportunity to make representations to the Court the Board should be able to keep itself informed of what is happening and to satisfy the Court that proper arrangements can and will be made for the accused person's admission and care. Each Board should establish standard arrangements and procedures for making representations to a Court.

Boards' Designated Officers

4.8   Each Area General Manager should designate an officer (referred to hereafter as the Designated Officer) to take responsibility for making the Board's representations in Court and advance arrangements for admission (paragraphs 4.16 to 4.21 and 4.24 of the Code), and, if admission is ordered, for ensuring that the admission is properly effected within the time available. In performing these duties the Designated Officer should co-operate with administrative staff at Area and Unit level and with professional staff including consultant psychiatrists and the Director of Public Health, all of whom should be notified of the identity of the Designated Officer and be prepared to co-operate with him in any case where admission by order of a Court is a possibility. The Designated Officer's identity should also be given to the Northern Ireland Court Service for notification to the Courts as their point of contact with the Board, to the Northern Ireland Office and to the Department.

Duties of the doctor giving medical evidence to the Court

4.9   The doctor is required, without prejudging the case, to give impartial professional evidence about the accused person's mental condition; whether that condition satisfies the criteria required in any of the Articles in Part III of the Order listed in paragraph 4.5 of the Code; and what arrangements would be appropriate for the accused person's further care. He could also be asked for advice as to how those arrangements could be put into practice.

4.10   In order to carry out these duties the doctor must be familiar with the provisions of Part III of the Order, and particularly the criteria for application of the Articles referred to in paragraph 4.5 of the Code. He must be able to make an adequate assessment of the accused person's mental state. To do this he must have access to relevant reports, including details of the accused person's previous psychiatric history and treatment, documents relating to the alleged offence and any relevant reports by other professionals such as social workers. He must have access to and examine the accused person and form an opinion on the most suitable provision for his future management.

Medical assessment of the accused person

4.11 If assessment has to be carried out in prison, the doctor giving evidence should make arrangements to obtain information about observations on the accused person's mental state while in prison and about any treatment given, and to gain access to the accused person. The approach will normally be to the Senior Medical Officer in the prison, and, if another psychiatrist has attended the accused person there, the doctor should consult him about his findings and any treatment that has been given. Before carrying out the examination the doctor should identify himself to the accused person and explain at whose request he is preparing his report.

Arrangements for the accused person's hospital care

4.12 If he concludes that hospital admission would be a proper and suitable provision for the accused person, the examining doctor, before giving his evidence to the Court, should ascertain whether admission can be arranged and the accused person given the care he needs. To that end the examining doctor should identify the hospital to which the accused person should be admitted and the consultant who will be in charge of his treatment. If the examining doctor is to be that consultant, he should consult his professional and administrative colleagues, including the Designated Officer, to ensure that they are agreed that admission would be feasible. If another consultant is to be responsible for the accused person's hospital care the examining doctor should confirm that the consultant concerned is in a position to admit the patient and arrange for his proper management. Before giving this confirmation, that consultant should consult his professional and administrative colleagues, including the Designated Officer, to ensure that they are agreed that admission would be feasible.

4.13 It is **particularly** important that nursing staff understand what is proposed so that they can make adequate preparation for the admission. If the examining doctor is to be the consultant in charge of the accused person's treatment, it would normally be good practice for him to arrange for a nursing colleague also to assess the accused person's suitability for care in the hospital identified. If another consultant is to be responsible for the accused person's hospital care, that consultant should consult his nursing colleagues before advising the examining doctor on the feasibility of managing the accused person in his unit. The Designated Officer should be kept fully informed of the professionals' decisions and his agreement obtained to their conclusions.

4.14 If the accused person appears to need facilities that are not available in Northern Ireland, the examining doctor should confirm that other satisfactory arrangements can be made. This applies where psychiatric care is needed in conditions of security which can only be provided in a special hospital in Scotland or England (paragraphs 4.27 to 4.29 of the Code).

4.15 It is particularly important, where there is a possibility that the Court may find the accused person unfit to be tried or not guilty on the grounds of insanity, that any doctor giving evidence should ensure that the consultant likely to be responsible for the accused person's care and the Board's Designated Officer are notified at the earliest possible stage.

Boards' representations in Court

4.16 In those cases where Boards must be given an opportunity to make representations, the Court will notify the Board's Designated Officer of the circumstances of the case and the date of the hearing. There should be prior understanding about which Board to notify. Usually this will be the Board for the area in which the accused person resides and will be clear from his home address. Where there is any uncertainty, the accused person should be asked where he usually lives in order to obtain a decision. The principle is that the accused person's perception of where he is resident (either currently or, failing that, most recently) is the criterion. Where an accused person cannot identify a current or recent address, the Board for the area in which the alleged crime was committed should accept responsibility. If the Court notifies the wrong Board, that Board should promptly refer the matter back to the Court for redirection and at the same time inform the appropriate Board that this is being done. Exceptionally, where admission to a hospital which is administered by another Board is proposed, the latter Board should make the representations to the Court. In such circumstances the Designated Officer of each Board should agree the way forward and explain the position to the Court.

4.17   Any notification of a case by a Court to a Board should be referred to the Board's Designated Officer. The Board's standard procedures for making representations to the Court should be put into effect by the Designated Officer and followed in any case where there is a possibility that the Court may order admission to hospital.

4.18   The Board's representative must be able to advise the Court what arrangements would be made for the accused person's admission to hospital and subsequent care should the Court decide to order admission. He may be either the Designated Officer or another officer so authorised by the Designated Officer. Where a consultant psychiatrist employed by the Board is giving evidence, that consultant may be the authorised officer. This would, however, probably not be a suitable arrangement where he was giving evidence to the effect that hospital admission would not be appropriate. In such circumstances, the Designated Officer should attend in person or send an authorised deputy. In any event the Designated Officer should, before the date of the hearing, give the name of the Board's representative to the Clerk of the Court.

4.19   If a consultant psychiatrist acts as the Board's representative he **must** obtain the Designated Officer's assurance that the Board endorses his proposals. Likewise, if the Designated Officer or another officer acts in this capacity, he **must** ensure that he has the agreement of the professional staff concerned to any arrangements in regard to which he may express the Board's acceptance. In particular he must consult with the psychiatrist giving evidence to ensure that the representations made on the Board's behalf are compatible with the medical proposals for the accused person's further management.

Arrangements for Admission

4.20   An order by a Court for admission must be implemented within a fixed time: 7 days for admission under Article 42 or 43; 28 days under Article 44, 45, 49 or 50.

4.21   The Court has no power to designate the hospital to which the patient is to be admitted. That is a matter for the Board after an order is made, though normally it will have been determined before the order is made. The Designated Officer in each Board will be responsible for ensuring that arrangements for the patient's reception are made by the appropriate professional and administrative staff. It is essential that these are made in advance so that if admission is ordered the patient can be admitted within the appropriate fixed time.

Admissions directed by the Secretary of State

4.22   The Secretary of State may direct that a person in custody be admitted to hospital under the following Articles of the Order. In practice admission will be directed by the Northern Ireland Office exercising the powers of the Secretary of State.

i. Articles 53 and 54 - Transfer directions.

The Secretary of State may direct the hospital admission of a person serving a sentence of imprisonment (Article 53) or of certain other persons who are in custody, most commonly those on remand (Article 54). The Secretary of State may also, and in some cases must, direct that the person removed to hospital should be subject to restrictions (Article 55). Written reports by a Part II doctor and by one other medical practitioner are required. These must specify that the person to be transferred is suffering from mental illness or severe mental impairment and that the nature or degree of the disorder is such to warrant his detention in hospital for medical treatment. In practice these reports are commonly made by a consultant psychiatrist in attendance at the prison and by a prison medical officer. The subject of a transfer direction must be admitted to hospital within 14 days of the date of the direction. The subject of a transfer direction has the same status as a person who is subject to a hospital order, and a restriction direction made by the Secretary of State has the same effect as a restriction order made by a Court under Article 47 (paragraph 4.5 iii of the Code).

ii. Article 52 - Persons ordered to be kept in custody during Her Majesty's pleasure.

This Article is seldom used in practice. It applies to servicemen whom Courts Martial have found unfit to plead or not guilty by reason of insanity. Medical evidence as to the serviceman's mental state is heard by the Court Martial, and no further medical evidence is required when the powers in Article 52 are being exercised. The subject of a direction under this Article has the same status as a person who is subject to a hospital order together with a restriction order without limitation of time made by a Court under Articles 44 and 47 (paragraph 4.5 iii of the Code).

4.23 The Order makes no provision for Board representation where the Secretary of State is considering hospital admission. In practice the Northern Ireland Office will ensure that the appropriate Board is adequately consulted and that professional staff of the Board are given an opportunity to assess the patient. The guidance in paragraphs 4.6 to 4.21 of the Code on examining the patient, agreeing a course of action and making representations should be applied as appropriate.

Admission

4.24 Once a Part III admission has been ordered, the Board should receive immediate formal notification. Court orders are given by the Court to the person directed to convey the patient to the hospital, and a copy will be sent to the Board's Designated Officer. A transfer direction is sent by the Northern Ireland Office to the governor of the prison where the person to whom the direction applies is being held. The Northern Ireland Office will at the same time send a copy of the direction to the Board's Designated Officer. If received by any other Board employee the orders and transfer directions should immediately be brought to the attention of the Designated Officer. The latter should ensure that arrangements for admission are finalised promptly so that the patient can be conveyed to hospital within the specified time.

Conveyance to hospital

4.25 A Court order or transfer direction is sufficient authority for the patient to be conveyed to hospital. Most Part III admissions are of persons in custody. In these circumstances the Board's Designated Officer should ensure that consultations take place between staff in the prison and the receiving hospital at an early date on the timing of the move and on any other practical details. In the unlikely event of an ASW being directed by the Court to convey the patient to hospital, the ASW should follow the guidance in paragraphs 2.40 to 2.49 of the Code, as appropriate.

4.26   A Court order or transfer direction is also the authority to detain the patient. Boards should ensure that the original order or direction is received. This should be delivered with the patient to the receiving hospital.

Admissions to special hospitals

4.27   A patient ordered by a Court or ordered by the Secretary of State to be detained in hospital may require treatment in conditions of security which are not available in Northern Ireland. The special hospitals in Great Britain provide psychiatric care in conditions of extra security, and patients from Northern Ireland may be admitted to these hospitals, provided the relevant authority in Great Britain agrees to their admission.

4.28   A Northern Ireland Court can only order admission to a hospital within its jurisdiction. If admission to a special hospital is necessary, the Court will order the appropriate Board to admit the patient to hospital, and that Board must seek authority, from the Department of Health and Social Services or the Northern Ireland Office, for his transfer to a special hospital. The necessary arrangements for the move must, therefore, be put in hand before representations are made to the Court. It is of vital importance in such cases that the Court should be advised that the patient cannot be accommodated in a Northern Ireland hospital, that transfer to a special hospital will be required, and of the prospects and likely timing of such a transfer.

4.29   The arrangements for the removal of a patient to a special hospital in Great Britain are complex as several different agencies are involved. Before a special hospital authority agrees to the admission of a patient from Northern Ireland, it is usual for a consultant from the special hospital to visit and assess the patient. Formal authorisation for the patient's removal to Great Britain must be obtained from the Department of Health and Social Services or, if a restriction order is made, the Northern Ireland Office. The original Court order or transfer direction and the original authorisation for removal (which will be sent to the Board's Designated Officer by the Department or the Northern Ireland Office) must accompany the patient, when he is transferred. Specific guidance has been issued to psychiatrists on the transfer of patients to special hospitals.

Admissions from special hospitals

4.30   The special hospitals accept patients from Northern Ireland on the understanding that these patients will return to Northern Ireland when they no longer require to be managed in conditions of high security. Normally such a patient will return to the hospital from which he was originally transferred, or to which he was originally committed pursuant to an order of a Northern Ireland Court or the Secretary of State. Authority for the patient's transfer from the special hospital is given by the Home Secretary or by the Secretary of State for Scotland. Before it is given, the relevant authority in Great Britain will seek formal confirmation from the Department, or the Northern Ireland Office, that arrangements have been made for the patient's admission to a Northern Ireland hospital.

4.31   The first approach is usually made by the responsible consultant in the special hospital to the Northern Ireland consultant who will be the RMO on the patient's return. The latter in turn has the responsibility for ensuring that the patient can be suitably managed under his care, for advising his Board that this is so, and for agreeing the timing and details of the transfer. That requires, firstly, an assessment of the patient's condition and of the requirements for his management in hospital. It is common practice, though not an absolute requirement, for an assessment visit to be made to the special hospital by the Northern Ireland consultant concerned, and, when this is done, a nursing colleague should accompany the visiting consultant. On return the consultant should confirm his assessment in writing to the special hospital consultant and inform the Board of his conclusions. It is helpful for his report to be copied to the Director of Public Health and to the Department's medical adviser on mental health. If the consultant is reporting to the Board that the patient can be properly managed under his care, he should confirm that his nursing colleagues are in agreement with that view.

4.32   When a detained patient is transferred to Northern Ireland the receiving hospital must ensure that the original Court order or transfer direction and the original authorisation for removal to Northern Ireland are received.

Guardianship ordered by a Court

4.33   As a potentially useful alternative to hospital orders, Courts are empowered (Article 44) to make guardianship orders where the prescribed criteria, which are similar to those applying to a hospital order, are met and the Court, having regard to all the circumstances, considers reception into the guardianship of the Board, or of any other person, appropriate. Guardianship orders may be particularly suitable in helping to meet the needs of some offenders who could benefit from occupation, training and education in the community. The Court's decision will be based on oral evidence by a Part II doctor, written or oral evidence from another medical practitioner and written or oral evidence from an ASW.

4.34 Before making such an order the Court has to be satisfied that the Board or other person is willing to act as guardian. The Board will need to be satisfied with the arrangements, and, in considering the appropriateness of guardianship, it will be guided by the same principles as apply under Part II of the Order. Similarly the powers and duties conferred on the Board or private guardian and the provisions as to duration, renewal and discharge are those which apply to Part II guardianship applications except that the power to discharge is not available to the nearest relative.

5. TREATMENT AND CARE

Introduction

5.1   The guidance in this chapter deals with the treatment and care, under medical supervision, of all mentally disordered patients. Specific guidance is given on particular aspects of treatment and care for patients in hospital. Where the guidance applies only to patients detained under the provisions of the Order, that is made clear in the text.

5.2   **As defined in Article 2(2) of the Order medical treatment "includes nursing, and also includes care and training under medical supervision".** This acknowledges that modern psychiatric care is a team activity involving several disciplines, including psychiatry, clinical psychology, nursing, occupational therapy and social work. The team approach need not undermine the professional independence of the various team members who will have their own professional codes of practice. However, it is necessary to reconcile the need for team involvement in patient care with continuing medical responsibility for the patient's clinical management. That responsibility is recognised in the term "responsible medical officer" (RMO), the doctor, appointed for the purposes of Part II of the Order by the Mental Health Commission, who is in charge of the assessment or treatment of the patient.

Principles of treatment

5.3   All treatment should:

- **be primarily for the benefit of the patient.** Where possible the patient's willing participation should be obtained. The main aims should be, so far as is possible, to improve health and reduce handicap including social handicap;

- **protect the safety of the patient and other people.** In the course of treatment or in the interests of safety, restriction of liberty may be necessary but should never be used as a punishment and should only be used as a last resort to the minimum extent necessary;

- **respect the patient's dignity and rights.** No treatment should deprive a patient of food, shelter, water, warmth, a comfortable environment or confidentiality;

- **respect the patient's rights to privacy and freedom of choice.** Forms of treatment, such as psychological treatment techniques, group therapy and behaviour modification programmes, which may intrude on the patient's normal right to privacy and freedom of action, should be carefully planned and conducted by experienced and appropriately trained staff and should be kept under review;

- **respect the patient's rights to information.** Patients are entitled to information and an explanation about their condition, any treatment which is proposed, and their rights. This information should be conveyed at a suitable time and in a form which takes account of the patient's capacity to understand.

These principles apply to the treatment of all mentally disordered patients whether or not they are in hospital. In hospital practice they apply to both voluntary and detained patients including those admitted under Part III of the Order.

Treatment Plans

5.4 Treatment plans are essential in order to observe the principles which are set out above and to ensure that the different elements of patient care are co-ordinated as parts of an effective programme. Detailed programmes of treatment and care by members of individual disciplines should be developed in accordance with the overall treatment plan and recorded in their respective notes.

5.5 In hospital, consultants should initiate the formulation of treatment plans which should be prepared in consultation with their professional colleagues. The plan should be recorded in the patient's clinical notes. It should include a description of the immediate and long-term goals for the patient with a clear indication of the treatments proposed and the methods of treatment. The patient's progress and possible changes to the plan should be reviewed at regular intervals. Wherever possible the plan should be discussed with the patient who should be encouraged to say whether or not he agrees with the plan and to make his own contribution. In many cases it will be important to discuss the plan with the patient's close relatives, and the patient's consent to this being done must be obtained whenever possible in keeping with the professionals' duty of confidentiality to their patients, and their respective codes of ethics.

5.6 In the community, the doctor in charge of the patient's treatment should initiate the formulation of the treatment plan along similar lines. Where a patient is being treated in the community by a consultant that consultant should normally take the lead. In any event, in such cases, the respective roles and responsibilities of the consultant and the patient's GP should be clearly understood and agreed.

5.7 Treatment takes many forms. Some, such as psychological treatment techniques, can be intrusive and interfere with the patient's rights. Such techniques should only be used when authorised, as part of the patient's agreed treatment plan, by the RMO following a full discussion with the professional staff concerned with the patient. They should not be used without the patient's consent except in carefully justified circumstances. If consent is not or cannot be given the RMO should seek the advice of a suitably qualified person who is not a member of the clinical team responsible for the patient. This would normally be a clinical psychologist experienced in the use of the intended techniques although some members of other professions may have suitable expertise and experience. The RMO may delegate appropriate members of staff to use such treatments. Where he does so, it is his responsibility to ensure that they are carried out only by staff competent to do so. Professional line managers must ensure that members of staff have received relevant training and that they know who to turn to for advice when necessary.

Consent to treatment

5.8 The common law, as it relates to consent to treatment, applies to all patients whether voluntary or detained, except where statute (for example Part IV of the Order) specifically overrides it. Consent is the voluntary and continuing permission of the patient for a particular form of treatment to be given, based on an adequate knowledge of its nature, purpose, and likely effects. The assessment of the patient's ability to make a decision about his own treatment and the nature and extent of the information to be given in seeking consent are matters for clinical judgment, guided by current professional practice and subject to legal requirements. Permission given under duress is not "consent". Being mentally disordered does not preclude the ability to give consent. The treatment proposed should be explained to the patient as fully as possible, in terms appropriate to his ability to understand. An explanation should be given of the desired effect and outcome of the treatment as well as of the risk of developing significant and, in particular, disabling side-effects. The explanation may also include an account of the likely progress of the illness if the treatment is not given. It should be explained to the patient that he has a right to withdraw consent at any time.

5.9 Part IV of the Order imposes conditions on giving treatment with or without consent. Article 63 of the Order provides that, for specified forms of treatment, consent **and** a second opinion are required and applies to **all** patients (paragraphs 5.10 and 5.11 of the Code). The provision of treatment to certain **detained** patients is dealt with in a number of Articles which need to be read together. Article 64 provides that, for the treatments specified, consent **or** a second opinion is required (paragraphs 5.12 and 5.13), and Article 69 provides that treatment may be given in certain cases without either the patient's consent or a second opinion. Article 62 provides that the powers in Article 64 and 69 of the Order to treat detained patients without consent do not apply to those liable to be detained by virtue of Article 7(2), 7(3), 42, 129 or 130, liable to be detained by virtue of directions under Article 46(4), or conditionally discharged under Article 48(2), 78 or 79. In circumstances where there is no specific legislative provision the common law applies. Even when consent is not legally required, every attempt should be made to explain what is proposed and to obtain the patient's agreement.

Treatment requiring consent and a second opinion

5.10 Under **Article 63** of the Order psychosurgery (any surgical operation for destroying the functioning of brain tissue) requires consent **and** a second opinion. As specified by Regulation 6 of the Mental Health (Nurses, Guardianship, Consent to Treatment and Prescribed Forms) Regulations (Northern Ireland) 1986, surgical implantation of hormones for the purposes of reducing male sexual drive also requires consent **and** a second opinion (paragraph 181 of the Guide).

5.11 The consent must be validated by a Part IV doctor (not being the RMO), and by 2 other persons (not being medical practitioners) appointed for the purpose by the Mental Health Commission (Article 63(2)(a) and paragraph 182 of the Guide). If they agree the consent is valid, they should complete Part I of Form 21. The Part IV doctor must also consider whether the proposed treatment is appropriate (paragraphs 183 and 184 of the Guide) and, if he is satisfied that it is, complete Part II of Form 21. The completed forms must be sent to the Mental Health Commission.

Treatment requiring consent or a second opinion

5.12 Article 64 of the Order applies to detained patients other than those excepted by Article 62 (paragraph 5.9 of the Code). Under Article 64 the administration of medicine 3 months or more after its first administration during any continuing period of liability for detention requires consent **or a** second opinion. As specified by Regulation 6 of the Mental Health (Nurses, Guardianship, Consent to Treatment and Prescribed Forms) Regulations (Northern Ireland) 1986 electro-convulsive therapy also requires consent **or** a second opinion. In the case of detained patients to whom Article 64 does not apply consent must be obtained.

5.13 In the case of consent given by a detained patient to which Article 64 applies, the consent must be validated by the RMO or a Part IV doctor (paragraph 187 of the Guide). Form 22 is used for this purpose. Where a valid consent is not or cannot be given, a second opinion must be obtained: in the case of electro-convulsive therapy from a Part IV doctor; and for the administration of medicine from either a Part II or Part IV doctor (paragraph 187 of the Guide). This is recorded on Form 23. The completed forms must be sent to the Mental Health Commission.

Treatment without consent

5.14 Article 69 of the Order applies to detained patients other than those excepted by Article 62 (paragraph 5.9 of the Code). Under Article 69 consent is not required for medical treatment (other than treatment falling within Articles 63 or 64) given to those patients for the mental disorder from which they are suffering, provided the treatment is given by or under the direction of the RMO. The exclusion of patients remanded under Article 42 should be noted. If a Court remands an accused person to hospital for assessment under that Article, no legal right to treat without consent is thereby conferred, and this will be relevant if a therapeutic trial of drugs is contemplated as part of the assessment process. In that case, unless the patient is willing to accept treatment, remand for treatment under Article 43 would be required.

5.15 For patients to whom Article 69 does not apply, including all patients not subject to detention, the legal position concerning treatment without consent derives from common law (which, of course, does not apply only or specifically to patients with mental disorder or treatment for mental disorder). Generally speaking consent is a legal pre-requisite of treatment except when the patient is incapable of giving consent because he is:

- a child with insufficient understanding and intelligence, in which case a parent or person having parental authority may consent;

- an adult suffering from mental handicap to a degree that renders him incapable of understanding;

- unconscious and in urgent need of treatment to preserve life, health or well-being (unless there is unequivocal and reliable evidence that the patient did not want that treatment) provided that the treatment has to be administered while the patient is still unconscious;

- suffering from a mental disorder leading to behaviour which is an immediate serious danger to himself or others, and the treatment is the minimum necessary to avert that danger but the provisions of the Order cannot be immediately invoked; or

- otherwise incapable and in need of medical care in circumstances in which he has not declared his unwillingness to be treated prior to the onset of the incapacitating condition.

5.16 In F v West Berkshire Health Authority and another (Mental Health Act Commission intervening) ([1989] 2 ALL ER 545), the House of Lords held that, in all cases involving the treatment of a person incapable of giving consent, the treatment must be "in the patient's best interest". It must be:

- necessary to save life or prevent a deterioration or ensure an improvement in the patient's physical or mental health;

- in accordance with a practice accepted at the time by a responsible body of medical opinion skilled in the particular form of treatment in question.

The standard of care required of the doctor concerned in all cases is that laid down in Bolam v Friern Hospital Management Committee ([1957] 1 WLR 582), namely, that he must act in accordance with a responsible and competent body of relevant professional opinion. Agreement of the nearest relative is desirable but not essential.

5.17 If repeated emergency drug treatment for mental disorder has to be given to a patient, without his consent, the responsible doctor should consider whether the patient's condition and the circumstances of the case might require that patient to be detained under the provisions of the Order.

5.18 In the above noted case, F v West Berkshire Health Authority and another (Mental Health Act Commission intervening), the House of Lords held that, as a matter of practice, sterilisation should not be performed on an adult who lacks the capacity to give consent without first obtaining the opinion of the High Court that the operation is, in the circumstances, in the best interests of the persons concerned. The Courts in Northern Ireland may apply that decision.

Consent by children and young persons under the age of 18 years

5.19 The guidance on admission to hospital of children and young persons under the age of 18 years applies also to the treatment of such patients (see paragraphs 2.31 to 2.36 of the Code). When treatment is being planned the following questions (in addition to those listed in paragraph 2.34) need to be asked:

- where a parent refuses consent to treatment, how sound are the reasons and on what grounds are they made?

- how necessary is treatment for the child?

- how feasible would be treatment of a child under the age of 16 years living at home if there was no parental consent and no statutory orders?

5.20 The following guidance applies to young people who are not detained under the Act:

> a. **Under 16**. Children under the age of 16 years who have 'sufficient understanding and intelligence' can take decisions about their own medical treatment in the same way as adults. Otherwise the permission of parents or guardians must be sought (save in emergencies when only the treatment necessary to end the emergency should be given). If the parents or guardians do not consent to treatment, consideration should be given to both the use of child care legislation and the Order before coming to a final conclusion as to what action should be taken. In complex cases wardship may be the preferable course to take for as long as wardship continues to exist.
>
> b. The same principles concerning consent apply in respect of children under the age of 16 years in the care of a Board. The legal authority to authorise any treatment is vested in the Board where a child in care, by virtue of a Court order, does not have 'sufficient understanding and intelligence' to take his own treatment decisions. The Board's legal obligation to consult the child's parents depends upon how the child was brought into care. Wherever possible, his parents should be consulted. Where a child is a ward of court, the consent of the High Court must be sought. In an emergency consent may be obtained retrospectively (but this should be regarded as wholly exceptional).
>
> c. **Young people aged 16 and 17**. Young people in this age group who have the capacity to make their own treatment decisions can do so in the same way as adults (Section 4 of the Age of Majority Act (Northern Ireland) 1969). Where such a young person does not have this capacity, the authorisation of either parent, guardian or care authority (whichever has the lawful authority in relation to the particular young person) must be obtained. The consent of the High Court must be obtained in the case of a ward of court.

5.21 The fact that a child or young person has been admitted as a voluntary patient by his parents or guardians should not lead professionals to assume that they have consented to any treatment regarded as 'necessary'. Consent should be sought for each aspect of the child's care and treatment as it arises. 'Blanket' consent forms must not be used.

Withdrawal of consent

5.22 A patient may withdraw consent at any time and where he does so the common law applies except where statute specifically overrides it. Article 66 of the Order provides that a patient may withdraw consent given by him in respect of treatment specifically requiring his consent under Article 63 or 64 of the Order before completion of the treatment. In such circumstances treatment must cease immediately:

- unless the RMO considers that its discontinuance would cause serious suffering to the patient (Article 68(2)); or

- until a second medical opinion is obtained in the case of a detained patient to whom Article 64 applies (paragraph 5.9 of the Code).

The patient should be kept informed of the intended course of action.

Urgent treatment

5.23 Urgent treatment may be given without the patient's consent if the circumstances make it impractical to obtain his consent and imperative to give treatment. In most cases the common law will apply (paragraph 5.15 of the Code). Article 68 of the Order makes provision for giving treatment covered by Articles 63 and 64 in cases of urgent necessity (paragraphs 193 and 194 of the Guide). Where a patient is given treatment under Article 68 the Mental Health Commission must be notified immediately by the RMO (Article 68(4) and paragraph 196 of the Guide).

Consent by relatives

5.24   Except for consent by a parent of an immature child (paragraphs 5.15 to 5.20 of the Code), consent by a patient's relative is not an acceptable legal alternative to consent by the patient. The fact that a relative may agree to treatment being given to the patient does not alter the requirements of the common law or of the Order.

Treatment for physical illness

5.25   It should be noted that the principles of common law apply not only to treatment for mental disorder but to medical or surgical treatment which may be required for mentally disordered patients.

Review of treatment

5.26   Where a patient is given treatment under Article 63 or 64, the RMO must report, in accordance with the provisions of Article 67 of the Order, to the Mental Health Commission on the treatment and the patient's condition (paragraphs 190 and 191 of the Guide). Article 67(3) of the Order provides that the Commission may at any time give notice to the RMO that a certificate authorising treatment under Article 63 or 64 shall no longer apply (paragraph 192 of the Guide). Thereafter the treatment may be continued only if the provisions of the appropriate Article have been complied with once again or, pending such compliance, if the RMO considers that the abrupt discontinuance of the treatment would cause serious suffering to the patient (Article 68(2)).

Conduct presenting particular problems of management

5.27   Hospital patients, both voluntary and detained, and patients outside hospital, may behave in such a way as to disturb, or be a risk to, others around them or those charged with their care. They may also be a danger to themselves. The guidance in the following paragraphs has general application but certain paragraphs apply specifically to hospital practice.

5.28   Behaviour giving rise to problems of management of patients can include:

- refusal to participate in treatment programmes;

- prolonged verbal abuse and threatening behaviour;

- destructive behaviour;

- self injurious behaviour;

- physical attack on others.

Causes of behaviour problems

5.29 Possible causes of behaviour problems include:

- type of mental disorder;

- boredom and lack of environmental stimulation;

- too much stimulation, noise and general disruption;

- overcrowding;

- an unsuitable mix of patients;

- antagonism, aggression or provocation on the part of others;

- low staffing levels;

- inappropriate attitudes on the part of staff.

General preventive measures

5.30   In addition to preventive measures documented in the individual care plan, much can be done to prevent behaviour problems by ensuring environmental factors giving rise to such problems are as far as possible eliminated and staff are adequately trained and supported. General measures which can be taken might include:

- monitoring the mix of patients;

- developing primary nursing (giving each patient an identified nurse who is responsible and accountable for his nursing care);

- giving each patient a defined personal space and secure locker for the safe keeping of possessions;

- organising the environment to provide quiet rooms, recreation rooms and visitors' rooms;

- consistent conformity to the individual care programme;

- keeping patients fully informed of what is happening and why;

- allowing patients opportunities to express their thoughts and feelings;

- ensuring that patients' complaints are dealt with quickly and fairly;

- ensuring, where appropriate, continuing contact with the community through access to a telephone and visitors;

- providing structured activities;

- encouraging energetic activities for younger patients.

Dealing with violence

5.31 Although much violence is preventable, it is inevitable that violent incidents will occur from time to time, and staff should be adequately prepared to deal with them. It is emphasised, however, that only the minimum degree of restraint which is necessary in the circumstances should be employed to contain the incident.

Restraint

5.32 Restraint may take many forms and may vary in degree from mild instruction to seclusion. The essence of restraint is to contain or limit a patient's freedom. The most common reasons for restraint are:

- physical assault;

- destructive behaviour;

- non-compliance with treatment;

- self harm or risk of physical injury by accident;

- extreme and prolonged over-activity likely to lead to physical exhaustion.

The basic principles which should underlie any methods which are aimed at reducing and eliminating unwanted behaviour are:

- by intervention, to reduce such behaviour;

- to review regularly any intervention as part of the patient's agreed treatment programme relating to his particular management problem.

Policy on physical restraint

5.33 Each Unit of Management should have a clear, written policy on the use of **all** forms of **physical** restraint, and, where appropriate, the recording, monitoring, reviewing and follow-up of the use of restraint. That policy should be made known to all staff. Physical restraint in the context of this guidance includes locked ward doors, time out and seclusion.

5.34 When physical restraint is used, a written report on the incident and the form of restraint used must be kept and submitted to line management.

5.35　All staff who are likely to be involved must be adequately trained in the use of the various forms of physical restraint. Appropriate training must be given by a qualified instructor.

5.36　Patients should not be deprived of appropriate day-time clothing during the day with the sole intention of restricting their freedom of movement nor should they be deprived of other aids necessary for their daily living in the absence of any danger to themselves or others, unless as part of a therapeutic programme.

5.37　Staff must try and get to know patients not only in order that the patient may gain confidence in them but also so that they can learn to recognise potential danger signs in patients and be able to diffuse the situation in time. They should have good communication skills and know when to intervene in certain potentially aggressive situations. Continuity of staffing is an important factor both in the development of professional skills and consistency in managing patients.

Procedural steps for physical restraint

5.38　In all cases where physical restraint is applied:

- assistance should be sought verbally or by call system;

- one member of the team should assume control of the incident;

- the patient should be approached where possible and encouraged to stop the behaviour, or to comply with a request;

- where possible an explanation should be given of the consequences of non compliance;

- other patients or people not involved should be asked to leave the area quietly.

5.39　Any attempt to restrain aggressive behaviour should, as far as the situation will allow, be non-physical such as verbal command or persuasion. Where non-physical methods have failed or the incident is of such significance as to warrant immediate action, physical restraint may be necessary.

Physical restraint should only be used as a last resort and never as a matter of course. It can be used in an emergency when there is the possibility that significant harm will occur if intervention is withheld.

5.40   Although the presence of a larger number of staff may avert the outbreak of violence, when actual physical restraint is imposed fewer but well briefed staff are likely to be more effective in controlling and restraining the patient.

5.41   The person or persons imposing physical restraint should:

> - constantly explain the reason for action and enlist the patient's voluntary co-operation as soon as possible;
>
> - make a visual check for weapons;
>
> - nominate staff members to assist in control and allocate each a specific task;
>
> - aim at restraining arms and legs to immobilise the patient simply and safely;
>
> - avoid neck holds;
>
> - avoid excess weight being placed on any area but particularly on the abdomen, chest or neck;
>
> - not slap, kick or punch.

5.42   Each incident involving the use of physical restraint should be discussed, as soon as possible and preferably within 48 hours, by the professionals responsible for the patient's treatment and care. The discussion should be informal, allowing the staff involved in the incident to express their feelings and evaluate the incident. If necessary modification should be made to the patient's treatment plan.

Personal searches

5.43   Each Unit of Management should draw up policy and procedural guidance relating to searching patients and their belongings, and the recording of searches. This guidance should be checked by a legal adviser and made

TREATMENT AND CARE

known to all staff who may be involved. Searches should only be carried out where there are lawful and necessary grounds for such action. The patient's consent should be obtained if possible. If it is not, the Unit General Manager or delegated senior staff should be consulted before more junior staff undertake a search. The nurse in charge of the ward should supervise staff undertaking the search.

5.44 The manner in which the search is conducted should ensure the greatest possible privacy and respect for the dignity of the patient. Only the minimum amount of force should be used, should the patient be difficult. Searches of a patient's person should only be done by a staff member of the same sex as the patient, unless urgent necessity dictates otherwise. If items belonging to the patient are removed, he should be told who has custody and responsibility for these items.

Locked ward doors on open wards

5.45 The management, security and safety of patients should, wherever practicable, be ensured by means of adequate staffing. Boards are responsible for trying to ensure that staffing is adequate to avoid the need for the practice of locking patients in wards or any other area solely for their containment.

5.46 The nurse in charge of the ward at any given time is responsible for the care and protection of the patients and staff and the maintenance of a safe environment. To maintain a safe environment he may find it necessary to lock ward doors, and there should be local detailed procedures for doing this. The nurse should:

- inform all staff of the reason why the action has been taken and how long it will last;

- inform the patient or patients whose behaviour has led to the locking of the ward door of the reason for taking such action;

- inform all other patients that they may leave on request at any time and ensure that someone is available to unlock the door;

- inform line management of the action taken;

- inform the consultant or his deputy of the action taken;

- keep a record of the action taken together with the reasons for the action;

- use the incident reporting procedures.

Time out

5.47 The Mental Health Commission has referred to "time out" as a behavioural procedure involving the removal of an individual from a rewarding to a non-rewarding situation for a short period of time as a consequence of behaviour which is specified as undesirable.

5.48 Time out is a planned therapeutic procedure and therefore should normally be part of the written treatment plan which should always specify the duration. It should be seen as one of a range of methods of managing difficult or disturbed patients and not as an immediate reaction to such behaviour. When time out is used, the course of the treatment should be regularly reviewed, the patient should be carefully monitored and a written record should be kept of observations.

Seclusion

5.49 The Mental Health Commission has referred to "seclusion" as the forcible denial of the company of other people by constraint within a closed environment. The patient is usually confined alone in a room, the door of which cannot be opened from the inside and from which there is no other means of exit open to the patient himself. The room should have adequate heating, lighting, ventilation and bedding.

5.50 Seclusion is an emergency management procedure for the short term control of patients whose behaviour is seriously disturbed and should be used as a last resort, after all other reasonable steps to control the behaviour have been taken. The sole aim in using seclusion is to contain severely disturbed behaviour which is likely to cause harm to others. It should never be used where there is a risk that the patient may take his own life. The decision to use seclusion can be made in the first instance by a doctor, the nurse in charge of the ward or a senior nurse manager. Where the decision is taken by someone other than a doctor, arrangements must be made for a doctor to attend immediately.

5.51 A nurse should be available within sight and sound of the seclusion room throughout the period of the patient's seclusion. The frequency of observation should be decided on an individual basis, but a documented report must be made every 15 minutes. The aim of observation is to monitor the state of the patient and to ascertain whether seclusion can be terminated. A patient who has been sedated should be kept under constant review.

5.52 If seclusion needs to continue, a review should be made in the seclusion room, every 2 hours by 2 nurses and every 4 hours by a doctor.

Special accommodation of dangerous patients

5.53 A small number of mentally disordered patients present such problems of violent, criminal or severely anti-social conduct that special arrangements are needed for their safe accommodation in hospital. Some, but not all, will be detained by order of a Court or the Secretary of State under Part III of the Order. Conditions of high security for such patients are provided in the special hospitals in England and Scotland. For patients presenting similar problems but to a lesser degree special accommodation is provided in High Intensive Nursing Care Units (HINCUs) in major psychiatric and mental handicap hospitals in Northern Ireland. The guidance in this Chapter is generally applicable in HINCUs. However, extra measures including locked wards have to be accepted in the interests of safety.

GLOSSARY

Applicant, the	The patient's nearest relative or an Approved Social Worker, or a person appointed by the County Court to act as the nearest relative.
Approved Social Worker (ASW)	A social worker specially trained in dealing with persons suffering from mental disorder, and appointed by a Board to act as an ASW for the purposes of the Order.
Board	A Health and Social Services Board
Department, the	The Department of Health and Social Services.
Forms (numbered)	The forms which are required to be prescribed under the Order. They are prescribed under the Mental Health (Nurses, Guardianship, Consent to Treatment and Prescribed Forms) Regulations (Northern Ireland) 1986 (SR 1986 No 174) as amended, and are included also in the Guide.
Guide, the	"The Mental Health (NI) Order 1986 - A Guide" published by the Department in 1986.
Medical treatment	Medical treatment is broadly defined to include nursing, and also care and training under medical supervision.
Mental disorder	This is defined in Article 3 of the Order, and discussed in paragraphs 8 to 14 of the Guide.
Mental Health Commission	The Mental Health Commission for Northern Ireland established under Article 85 of the Order to perform specified statutory functions.
Mental Health Review Tribunal	Appeal tribunal constituted in accordance with Article 70 of the Order.

Nearest relative	This is defined in Article 32 of the Order by reference to a list of relationships, a caring relative taking priority over a non-caring relative, whatever his position on the list. The list is also reproduced in the notes to the relevant prescribed forms.
Order, the	The Mental Health (Northern Ireland) Order 1986.
Part II/Part IV Doctor	A medical practitioner appointed by the Mental Health Commission for the purposes of these Parts of the Order.
Patient	A person suffering or appearing to be suffering from mental disorder. (NB A different meaning applies for the purposes of Part VIII of the Order).
Responsible Board	For a hospital patient, the Board administering the hospital. For guardianship, the Board for the area in which the patient resides.
Responsible Medical Officer (RMO)	The Part II doctor in charge of the patient's assessment or treatment (or who provides certain medical recommendations required by the Order for the purposes of guardianship).
Regulations	A number of regulations (also known as Statutory Rules) have been made under powers given in the Order. The most important, for the purposes of this Code, are the Mental Health (Nurses, Guardianship, Consent to Treatment and Prescribed Forms) Regulations (Northern Ireland) 1986, as amended.

INDEX OF STATUTORY REFERENCES

Age of Majority Act (Northern Ireland) 1969

Section
4   5.20

Mental Health Act 1983   1.14

Mental Health (Northern Ireland) Order 1986

Article	
2	1.5, 2.22, 5.2
3	1.10, 1.12
4	2.3, 2.22, 3.22
5	2.3, 2.7, 2.17, 2.48, 2.59
6	2.3, 2.21, 2.70
7	2.3, 2.64-2.66, 5.9
8	2.3, 2.37, 2.48, 2.50, 2.51
9	2.51, 2.57, 2.63
10	2.2
11	2.4, 2.54, 2.62
12	2.3, 2.63, 3.22
13	2.3
18	3.5, 3.15, 3.16
19	3.5, 3.6, 3.17
20	3.5
21	3.5, 3.19
22	3.18, 3.21
24	3.20
25	3.20
27	2.72, 3.20
28	3.20, 3.23
29	3.21

Article	
32	2.8, 3.7
36	2.7, 2.17, 3.6
40	2.13, 2.18, 2.29, 3.12
42	4.5, 4.6, 4.20, 5.9, 5.14
43	4.5, 4.6, 4.20, 5.14
44	4.5, 4.6, 4.20, 4.22, 4.33
45	4.5, 4.6, 4.20
46	5.9
47	4.5, 4.22
48	5.9
49	4.5, 4.6, 4.20
50	4.5, 4.6, 4.20
52	4.22
53	4.22
54	4.22
55	4.22
62	5.9
63	1.1, 5.9, 5.10, 5.11, 5.14, 5.22, 5.23, 5.26
64	5.9, 5.12, 5.13, 5.14, 5.22, 5.23, 5.26
66	5.22
67	5.26
68	5.9, 5.22, 5.23, 5.26
69	4.5, 5.9, 5.14, 5.15
78	5.9
79	5.9
111	1.1, 1.4
125	3.21
129	2.6, 5.9
130	5.9
131	2.38
132	2.38

Mental Health (Nurses, Guardianship, Consent to Treatment and Prescribed Forms) Regulations (Northern Ireland) 1986

Regulation
3	2.53, 2.66
4	3.20
5	3.20
6	5.10, 5.12
7	1.7

Mental Health (Nurses, Guardianship, Consent to Treatment and Prescribed Forms) (Amendment) Regulations (Northern Ireland) 1992

1.7

Mental Health (Scotland) Act 1984

1.14

INDEX

Admission

- alternatives 2.27-2.30
- applicant 2.7
- application 1.10, 2.2, 2.4-2.26, 2.64-2.71
- ASW's role 2.5, 2.6, 2.10, 2.11, 2.13-2.20, 2.56
- children and young persons 2.31-2.36
- Court order 4.5-4.21, 4.24, 4.27-4.29
- conveyance to hospital 2.37-2.49, 4.25
- criteria 2.22
- GP's role 2.12, 2.21, 2.70, 3.14, 5.6 *see also* recommending doctor's role
- hospital doctor's role 2.57-2.60, 2.64, 2.65, 2.69
- hospital nurse's role 2.52-2.56, 2.66-2.69
- medical examination 2.57-2.61
- nearest relative's role 2.8-2.12
- procedure 2.51-2.61
- recommending doctor's role 2.5, 2.6, 2.9, 2.10, 2.19, 2.21-2.25, 2.26-2.28, 2.70
- Secretary of State direction 4.4, 4.22, 4.23
- voluntary 2.27
- voluntary hospital patient 2.64-2.71

Assessment

- application *see* **Admission**
- period 2.58, 2.59, 2.63

ASW

- admission 2.7, 2.9-2.20, 2.26-2.30, 2.56
- conveyance to hospital 2.37, 2.38, 2.40-2.50, 4.25
- guardianship 3.5, 3.10-3.13, 3.16, 3.17, 4.33

Board

- admission 2.33, 2.59, 4.24, 5.20
- conveyance to hospital 2.37, 2.40, 2.48, 2.50, 4.25, 4.26
- Court order 4.1, 4.5-4.8, 4.16-4.19
- Designated Officer 4.8, 4.12, 4.13, 4.16-4.19, 4.21, 4.24, 4.25, 4.29
- guardianship 3.4, 3.16, 3.19, 3.20, 3.21, 3.23, 4.33, 4.34
- guidance 2.12, 2.33, 2.50, 3.20
- notification 2.51, 2.58, 2.61-2.63, 2.71, 3.18
- Secretary of State direction 4.23, 4.24
- special hospitals 4.28, 4.29, 4.31

Children and young persons

- admission 2.31-2.36
- consent to treatment 5.19-5.21

Consent

- children and young persons 5.19-5.21
- disclosure of information 2.28, 5.5
- meaning 5.8
- Mental Health Commission review 5.26
- personal searches 5.43
- relative 5.24
- treatment 5.9-5.13
- treatment without 5.14-5.18, 5.23
- withheld or withdrawn 3.21, 4.5, 5.7, 5.8, 5.22

Conveyance to hospital

- authority 2.37, 2.38, 4.25
- ASW's role 2.40-2.49
- GP's role *see* recommending doctor's role
- nearest relative's role 2.39
- person in custody 4.25
- recommending doctor's role 2.25, 2.39, 2.40
- sedated patient 2.49

Court

- admission ordered 4.5-4.21, 4.24, 4.27-4.29
- appointment of acting nearest relative 2.7, 2.17, 3.6, 3.10
- Board representation 4.5-4.8, 4.16-4.19, 4.34
- guardianship ordered 4.33, 4.34
- medical evidence 4.5, 4.9-4.12, 4.33

Criminal proceedings *see* **Court, Secretary of State**

Department of Health and Social Services

- Code of Practice 1.1, 1.3, 1.5
- delegated functions 4.1, 4.6
- Guide to Order 1.4
- special hospital 4.28-4.31

Designated Officer

- admission 4.20, 4.21, 4.24, 4.25
- Court cases 4.8, 4.12, 4.13, 4.16-4.19
- special hospital 4.29

Doctor

- Board representative in Court 4.18, 4.19
- conveyance to hospital 2.37, 2.39, 2.40, 2.49
- evidence in Court 4.5, 4.9-4.15
- examining 2.35, 2.55, 2.57, 2.58, 2.60-2.63, 3.14, 4.9-4.14
- GP 2.12, 2.21, 2.70, 3.14, 5.6 *see also* recommending
- guardianship 3.14, 4.33
- holding power 2.64, 2.65
- hospital 2.55, 2.57, 2.64-2.66, 2.68-2.70, 5.17, 5.50, 5.52
- Part II 1.16, 1.17, 2.3, 2.37, 2.57, 2.60, 2.63, 3.14, 4.5, 4.22
- Part IV 1.16, 5.11, 5.13
- prison 4.11, 4.22
- recommending 2.6, 2.9, 2.10, 2.19-2.30, 2.39, 2.40, 2.55, 2.60, 2.70
- RMO 1.17, 2.57-2.59, 2.63, 4.5, 5.2, 5.7, 5.11, 5.13, 5.14, 5.22, 5.23, 5.26
- special hospitals 4.29, 4.31
- standards 5.16

Documentation

- notification to Board 2.58, 2.61, 2.71
- notification to Mental Health Commission 2.61, 2.62, 2.71
- prescribed forms 1.7, 2.61, 2.71
- rectification 2.4, 2.62
- scrutiny 2.52-2.56

Guardianship

- applicant 3.6
- application 3.5-3.17
- ASW's role 3.5, 3.6, 3.10-3.13, 3.16, 3.17, 4.34
- Board's role 3.16, 3.19, 3.20, 4.34
- Court order 4.33, 4.34
- GP's role 3.14 *see also* recommending doctors' roles
- guardian's role 3.3, 3.21-3.24
- nearest relative's role 3.7-3.10
- purpose 3.1
- recommending doctors' roles 3.14, 3.15

Health and Social Services Board *see* Board

Holding power

- doctors 2.64, 2.65
- nurses 2.66-2.69

Management

- patient 4.10, 4.12, 4.19, 4.31, 5.2, 5.27-5.53
- staff 2.67

Mental disorder

- admission criteria 2.22
- cause of behaviour problem 5.29
- definition 1.10-1.14
- treatment 5.14, 5.15, 5.17, 5.25, 5.53

Mental Health Commission

- appointments 1.16, 5.2
- notification 2.51, 2.61, 2.62, 2.71, 3.18, 3.19, 3.20, 5.11, 5.13, 5.23
- review of treatment 5.26
- seclusion 5.49
- time out 5.47

Mental Health Review Tribunal

- application 3.20

Nearest Relative

- acting 2.7, 2.17, 3.6, 3.10
- advice 2.9, 2.10, 2.20, 2.23, 2.28, 2.29, 3.8
- applicant 2.7-2.13, 2.26, 2.29, 2.59, 3.6-3.10, 3.12, 3.16
- assistance 2.9, 2.12, 2.40, 3.8
- conveyance to hospital 2.39, 2.40
- definition 2.8, 3.7
- guardianship 3.3, 3.6-3.10, 3.12, 3.16, 3.17, 3.20, 4.34
- information 2.16, 2.48, 3.17
- objection 2.17, 3.10
- rights 2.16, 2.29, 3.20

Nurse

- admission role 2.46, 2.52, 2.53, 2.55
- community mental handicap 2.19, 2.28
- community psychiatric 2.19, 2.28
- conveyance to hospital 2.49
- holding power 2.66-2.69
- locked ward doors 5.46
- patient care 5,30
- personal searches 5.43
- seclusion 5.50-5.52
- training 5.30

Patient

- admission 2.51-2.61, 4.12, 4.21-4.24
- application for assessment 2.4-2.30
- application for guardianship 3.5-3.18, 3.25
- behavioural problems 5.27-5.30
- consent to treatment 5.8-5.24
- conveyance to hospital 2.37-2.50, 4.25, 4.26
- definition 1.15
- detention 2.63-2.69
- guardianship 3.20-3.24
- physical restraint 5.36-5.53
- rights 1.9, 2.72, 3.20
- treatment 5.1-5.7

Restraint

- discharge 1.8
- locked ward doors 5.45-5.46
- physical 5.33-5.42
- seclusion 5.49-5.52
- special accommodation 5.53
- time out 5.47, 5.48
- use 5.31-5.36

Searches

- personal 5.43-5.44

Special hospital

- admission from 4.30-4.32
- admission to 4.27-4.29
- Court order 4.14, 4.27-4.29

Secretary of State

- Admission 4.4, 4.22, 4.23
- Restriction 4.5, 4.22

Treatment

- children and young persons 2.32-2.34, 5.19-5.21
- consent 5.8-5.25
- court order 4.5, 4.6, 4.10-4.13, 4.27
- definition 5.1, 5.2
- detention for 2.2, 2.3, 2.60, 2.61, 2.63
- guardianship 2.1-3.4, 3.21, 3.22
- Mental Health Commission notification 2.61, 5.26
- plans 5.4-5.7, 5.48
- principles 1.8, 1.9, 5.3
- prison 4.3
- psychological 5.3, 5.7
- review 5.26, 5.32, 5.42
- RMO 5.2, 5.7, 5.13, 5.14, 5.22, 5.23, 5.26
- special hospital 4.27
- urgent 5.23
- voluntary patient 2.66